Teddy Bears
IN CROSS STITCH
OVER 30 ADORABLE DESIGNS

David and Charles

www.mycraftivity.com

A DAVID & CHARLES BOOK
Copyright © David & Charles Limited 2008

David & Charles is an F+W Publications Inc. company
4700 East Galbraith Road
Cincinnati, OH 45236

First published in the UK in 2008

Text and designs copyright © Sue Cook, Claire Crompton, Joan Elliott,
Michaela Learner, Joanne Sanderson and Lesley Teare 2008

Photography, illustrations and layout copyright © David & Charles 2008

Sue Cook, Claire Crompton, Joan Elliott, Michaela Learner, Joanne Sanderson and Lesley Teare
have asserted their right to be identified as authors of this work in accordance with the Copyright,
Designs and Patents Act, 1988.

A catalogue record for this book is available from the British Library.

ISBN-13: 978-0-7153-2933-7 hardback
ISBN-10: 0-7153-2933-2 hardback

ISBN-13: 978-0-7153-2938-2 paperback
ISBN-10: 0-7153-2938-3 paperback

Printed in China by RR Donnelley
for David & Charles
Brunel House   Newton Abbot   Devon

Senior Commissioning Editor: Cheryl Brown
Desk Editor: Bethany Dymond
Project Editor and Chart Preparation: Lin Clements
Art Editor: Charly Bailey
Production Controller: Ros Napper
Photographer: Kim Sayer

Visit our website at www.davidandcharles.co.uk

David & Charles books are available from all good bookshops; alternatively you can contact our
Orderline on 0870 9908222 or write to us at FREEPOST EX2 110, D&C Direct, Newton Abbot, TQ12 4ZZ
(no stamp required UK only); US customers call 800-289-0963 and Canadian customers call 800-840-5220.

Contents

Introduction

Teddy bears have been part of our lives for over 100 years, and their popularity never seems to wane. For most of those years they have been the childhood symbol of affection and love and this delightful cross stitch collection celebrates their special place in our lives.

There are traditional cuddly teddies, all-action circus teddies, ever-hungry kitchen teddies, romantic sweetheart teddies and a whole host of fun teddy friends. There are also lots of illustrated ideas throughout suggesting other ways to use the designs.

You might want to start your teddy bear stitching with four charming, traditional-style bears, reflecting the best of teddy bear making, each in a seasonal setting among pretty floral motifs.

If you love making up stories for the young ones in your life, then meet the Bugbears – Henry Honeybear, Lulu Ladybird and Betsy Butterfly – and let your imagination fly as you stitch these delightful designs.

Bright and busy circus bears, including clowns, acrobats, jugglers and trapeze artists, have been used to adorn a really useful alphabet with 26 bright and bold designs perfect for creating gifts for children and for adorning all sorts of accessories.

There must be hundreds of reasons why we love teddy bears and six endearing sentiments on a cheerful wall hanging express some loving thoughts about these charming companions. The six bears can also be used alone to create many smaller projects.

Some teddies in the kitchen are doing what bears do best – preparing, eating and, most of all, enjoying their food, especially sweet treats, and the fun designs are perfect for bringing humour and colourful decoration to the most

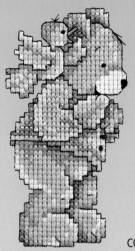

important room in the house. As the bears say, pudding

certainly does make life bearable!

Teddy bears and children are the perfect

combination: soft and cuddly, loving and loyal. The

comfort that a cherished bear can bring to a small child (and

us big ones too) never seems to dim. No nursery is complete without a teddy

friend and these utterly charming designs are perfect to welcome a new

baby into the world.

Teddy bears have a place in our hearts throughout the

whole year and a cheerful collection of calendar teddies,

one for each month, will help you celebrate seasonal

occasions with friends and family.

Finally, eight gorgeous sweetheart bears bring heartfelt

messages in a chapter full of designs for sending love and affection at

any time of year – for birthdays, anniversaries, Christmas, Valentine's Day and a host

of other occasions.

The teddy bear cross stitch designs in this book are colourful, endearing and versatile and can be used for so many

projects. The delightful designs will appeal to the whole family, inviting

you to create some memorable, hand-crafted cards, gifts, keepsakes

and decorations for your home, and in the process remind you just

how special teddies are. So cuddle up with some teddy bears

and get stitching.

Teddy Bear Seasons

Designed by Lesley Teare

Teddy bear toys have been popular for over 100 years,

and our affection for them never seems to wane. This chapter

features a collection of vintage bears, each dressed to reflect the period in

which they were designed. There are four in all, one for each of the year's seasons.

During the 1920s John was the most popular boy's name and our spring teddy

looks just like a John ought to – sturdy and dependable. He is gentle of course, as

all teddy bears are. Mary, the favourite name of the 1930s, is our summer bear and

is dressed in a check pinafore and a pretty bow. She is a sweet and loving bear who

adores sunshine and wild flowers. James was a popular boy's name in the 1950s and

our winter bear, full of mischief and ready to play, wears a warm scarf and pullover. He

looks ready for any adventure. Our 1990s bear is Michael, whose kind face invites you

to play in the autumn-ripe fields. His fur is silky soft and perfect for cuddles.

Each of the teddies is surrounded by pretty floral motifs, which could also be

used for project ideas – see overleaf and pages 13 and 17.

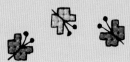

In this chapter four utterly charming bears celebrate each season from times past. The Spring Bear, shown here, is accompanied by bluebells, primroses and sweet Easter chicks.

Seasonal Bears

Aren't these four little bears delightful? Their clothes reflect the era that inspired them and each bear is surrounded by a pretty border of flowers, which could be used to create other projects – see below and pages 13 and 17 for ideas. There are some alphabets and numbers charted on page 75 which could be used for names and messages to personalize the designs.

STITCH COUNT (each design)
98h x 98w

DESIGN SIZE (each design)
18 x 18cm (7 x 7in)

MATERIALS (for each picture)
✿ 30.5 x 30.5cm (12 x 12in) 14-count white Aida
✿ Tapestry needle size 24
✿ DMC stranded cotton (floss) as listed in chart key
✿ Suitable picture frame

---

1 Prepare your fabric for work and mark the centre (see page 98). Follow the charts on pages 10–16 and begin stitching from the centre of the chart and centre of the fabric. Note that some of the colours use more than one skein – see chart key for details.

2 Work over one block of Aida and use two strands of stranded cotton (floss) for full and three-quarter cross stitches. Use two strands for French knots and then one strand for backstitch.

3 When the embroidery is complete remove any guide lines, press the work (see page 99) and then frame as desired (see page 101) or make up in some other way of your choice.

Bearing Gifts...

These teddy designs are very versatile – stitch the whole design or just the teddy or some of the flowers. For example, create a pretty bookmark, as shown here, by stitching just the flowers from the Spring Bear. If Aida or linen band is used, there will only be two edges to hem.

The Autumn Bear is a modern 1990s bear but is still quite at home at harvest time among poppies and wheat stalks. If you are short on time you could stitch just the bear and the poppies at his feet.

Spring Bear
DMC stranded cotton
Cross stitch (2 strands)

155	351	728	782 (2 skeins)	898	
310	− 703	• 742	/ 783	905	
333	✕ 726	772 (2 skeins)	798	/ 938	
L 349	727	I 780	○ 799		

Backstitch (1 strand)
—— 938

French knots (2 strands)
● 310
● 905

Teddy bears made during the 1920s were intended to look realistic,
with long noses, large feet and short limbs. Mohair was still
the favourite material for making bears. Kapok began to be used
for fillings as it was light and hygenic.

Summer Bear
DMC stranded cotton
Cross stitch (2 strands)

■ 310	436	742	**I** 826
⊙ 433	**U** 437	**I** 746	**** 827
434	**✕** 725	813	**—** 702
╱ 435	727 (3 skeins)	825	703

• 3865
(2 skeins)

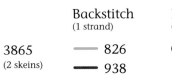

Backstitch
(1 strand)
— 826
— 938

French knots
(2 strands)
● 310

Bearing Gifts...

This lovely, sunny teddy design based on a 1930s bear would be perfect for a summer birthday. Why not stitch the design on a sky blue Aida or linen, mount it into a lemon-coloured double-fold card and decorate with some daisy buttons?

Autumn Bear

DMC stranded cotton

Cross stitch (2 strands)

■ 310	I 703	+ 813	976 (2 skeins)
347	O 728	826	× 977
\ 349	L 742	827 (2 skeins)	3826
351	/ 783	905	3827

Backstitch (1 strand)

— 938

French knots (2 strands)

● 310

The 1990s saw a new approach to bear-making, with teddy bear
'artists' making quality bears in limited editions for exclusive
outlets. This autumn teddy is still a traditional bear but with
a more friendly, expressive look and greater individuality.

Winter Bear

DMC stranded cotton

Cross stitch (2 strands)

162	351	729	/ 799	• 3865	
■ 310	U 676	\ 746	◉ 869		
347	I 703	772	905		
— 349	727	798 (2 skeins)	3829 (2 skeins)		

Backstitch
(1 strand)

— 938

— 975

French knots
(2 strands)

◉ 742

 *Bearing Gifts...*

This cosy teddy design based on a 1950s bear would be perfect for a seasonal card. You could stitch it on a sparkly Aida, stick it on to a shiny sapphire blue single-fold card and glue on gold braid to frame the design. Create a Christmas message with rub-on or stick-on letters.

Meet the Bugbears

When my son was very small he loved me making up stories just

for him. Our favourite walk used to take us past an old house with a

rather mysterious walled garden, which we sometimes glimpsed through a

tiny door. We decided it must be a magic place, full of interesting characters and so

the Bugbears came to life.

Henry Honeybear liked to think he was very efficient and busied himself

gathering flower nectar for honey. Ballerina Betsy was more interested in looking

pretty and flitted about keeping all the flowers in the garden looking pretty too.

Lulu was practical and artistic and spent her time putting the spots on ladybirds

with her little pot of black paint.

Almost 25 years later my son found the drawings I'd done to illustrate our

stories and I decided to chart them for cross stitch. So I hope you enjoy these

characters as much as we did. The designs are shown here as pictures but you can

use them to decorate many other items – see page 20–21 for some ideas.

These three delightful bugbears are sure to become firm favourites: meet Betsy Butterfly, Henry Honeybear and Lulu Ladybird.

Bugbear Pictures

These three fun bugbears designs are all worked in attractive shades and are very simple to stitch. Stitch them for the little girl or boy in your life and see what stories you can make up about these sweet characters.

STITCH COUNT (each design)
90h x 70w

DESIGN SIZE (each design)
16.5 x 12.7cm (6½ x 5in)

MATERIALS (for each picture)
❀ 24.5 x 20.3cm (11 x 8in)
   14-count white Aida
❀ Tapestry needle size 24
❀ DMC stranded cotton (floss)
   as listed in chart key
❀ Suitable picture frame

1 Prepare your fabric for work and mark the centre (see page 98). Follow the charts on pages 22–26 and begin stitching from the centre of the chart and centre of the fabric.

2 Work over one block of Aida and use two strands of stranded cotton (floss) for full and three-quarter cross stitch and French knots and then one strand for backstitch.

3 When the embroidery is complete remove any guide lines, press the work (see page 99) and then frame as desired (see page 101) or make up in some other way of your choice.

Over the last century teddy bears have featured in many well-known stories, with enduringly popular characters such as Rupert Bear, Winnie-the-Pooh and Paddington Bear. Rupert Bear's adventures with his friends in Nutwood began in 1920, when the cartoon character first appeared in the Daily Express newspaper.

Bearing Gifts...

These teddy designs have a timeless charm and would be perfect to adorn many items for gifts and keepsakes as suggested here and opposite. Alphabets and numbers charted on page 75 could be used to personalize the designs.

Make a lovely picture for a young child's room by stitching all three bugbears on one piece of fabric and mount in a brightly coloured frame. You could omit the stitching for the heart frames so all three friends appear together in the picture.

For
a keen ballerina,
stitch Betsy Butterfly
and attach the embroidery as
a patch on a pretty bag, perhaps
to hold ballet shoes, all ready for
dance class. Hem the edges of the
embroidery and glue it to the bag.
Glue trimming around the edge
and add a heart button as a
nice finishing touch.

Stitch
Lulu Ladybird for
a great room sign. Glue
the embroidery to patterned
felt and glue the felt on to thick
card. Turn the edges to the back and
glue. Stick a ribbon loop on the back
and neaten the back by gluing on plain
felt. Add a ric-rac trim and some
buttons. Use stick-on letters to
add a name on a piece
of card.

Stitch
Henry Honeybear
on finer 18-count Aida to
create a smaller design. Mount
the embroidery into a brightly
coloured double-fold card and
decorate with a length of gingham
ribbon or other bold embellishment.
Add a birthday greeting above or
below the design using stick-on
or rub-on letters.

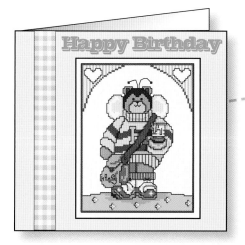

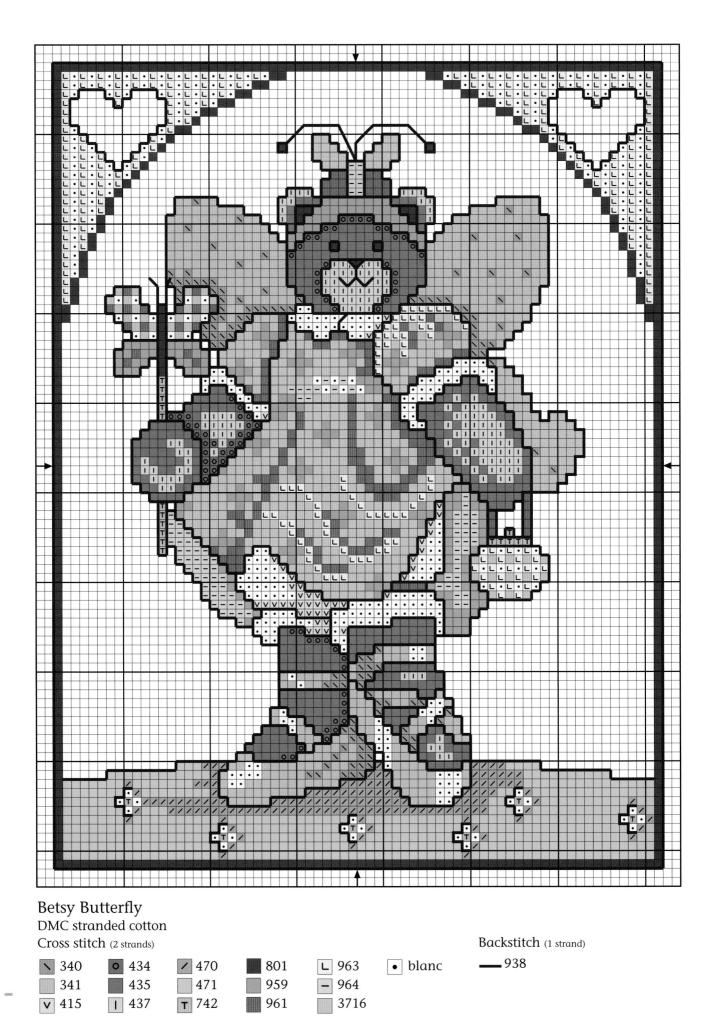

Betsy Butterfly
DMC stranded cotton

Cross stitch (2 strands)

340	o 434	/ 470	801	L 963	• blanc		
341	435	471	959	- 964			
v 415	I 437	T 742	961	3716			

Backstitch (1 strand)

— 938

A teddy bear collector is called an arctophile,
derived from two Greek words, arcos for bear
and philos for love.

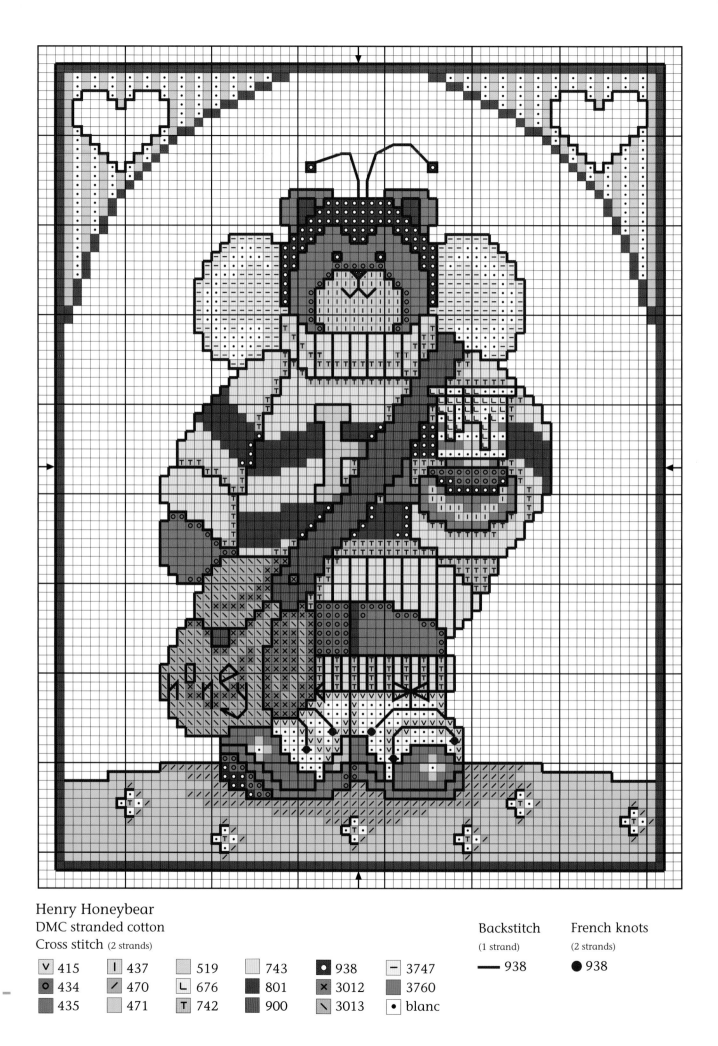

Henry Honeybear
DMC stranded cotton
Cross stitch (2 strands)

V 415	I 437	519	743	● 938	− 3747	
○ 434	∕ 470	L 676	801	✕ 3012	3760	
435	471	T 742	900	＼ 3013	• blanc	

Backstitch (1 strand) —— 938

French knots (2 strands) ● 938

*A collection of teddy bears is, very
appropriately, known as a 'hug'.*

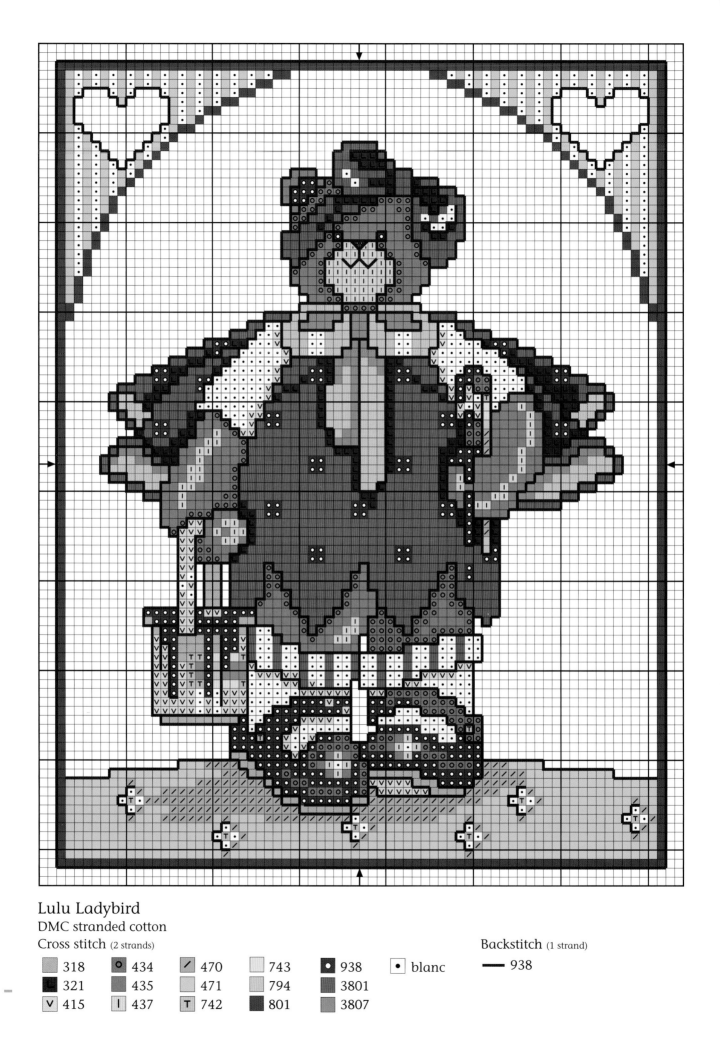

Lulu Ladybird

DMC stranded cotton

Cross stitch (2 strands)

Backstitch (1 strand)

	318	○	434	╱	470		743	○	938	•	blanc
■	321		435		471		794		3801			
V	415	I	437	T	742		801		3807			

— 938

The highest price paid, so far, for a teddy bear was an
astonishing £110,000 ($220,000) in 1994 for a
Steiff 'Teddy Girl' bear, originally made in 1904.

Circus Bears

Designed by Michaela Learner

Circuses have been touring the world for centuries – entertaining

spectacles full of dare-devil stunts, clowning comedy, loud music and

razzmatazz. Children in particular love the colour and excitement of the

circus and this chapter has 26 fun circus bears they will adore.

These teddies are up to all sorts of tricks as they decorate the letters of the alphabet.

There are clowns, acrobats, jugglers, trapeze artists and of course, the ring master.

The colours are bold and bright – perfect for gifts for children. The letters are just the

right size to be used as initials, names or messages of your choice and the four projects

shown give you some idea of how the letters might be used. A toy bag and play cube

are shown opposite, with a notebook, pen pot and baby's bib on the following pages.

Many of the motifs could also be stitched without their letter, perhaps for

birthday cards. For a larger project that would make a wonderful keepsake you could

stitch all of the letters arranged together as a sampler and framed as a picture.

There is all the fun of the circus to be found in this chapter with 26 versatile and colourful teddy designs, which children are sure to love.

Toy Bag

This bag is perfect for a child's room and can be used for toys, books or sleep wear. The size of the bag shown is 42 x 52cm (16½ x 20½in) but you can easily change the dimensions.

STITCH COUNT
(for design shown)
45h x 183w
DESIGN SIZE
8.3 x 33cm (3¼ x 13in)

MATERIALS
- ✿ 23 x 46cm (9 x 18in) 14-count white Aida
- ✿ Tapestry needle size 24–26
- ✿ DMC stranded cotton (floss) as listed in chart key
- ✿ Coats Ophir thread 300 gold
- ✿ 46 x 106.5cm (18 x 42in) medium to heavyweight print fabric
- ✿ Sewing thread to match print fabric
- ✿ Red cord 1.5m (2yd)
- ✿ Safety pin and dress-making pins
- ✿ Clear nail varnish or fray check fluid

1 Prepare your fabric for work and mark the centre (see page 98). Follow the charts on pages 34–41 and begin stitching from the centre of the chart and fabric. Allow one Aida block between letters. If creating another word, plan the letters on graph paper and count the overall number of stitches across the height and width. See page 98 for calculating the finished size of a design.

2 Work over one block of Aida and use two strands of stranded cotton (floss) for full and three-quarter cross stitches. Use two strands for any French knots and one strand for backstitches.

3 Prepare the band by counting up seven blocks from the top and bottom of the stitching and folding the excess Aida to the back on both long edges (overlapping in the middle). Tack in place. This fabric will prevent the print fabric from showing through. Fold the print fabric in half, wrong sides together, measure up 12cm (5in) from the fold line and place a couple of pins to make a line. Open up the fabric. Place the band with the lower edge on the pins, tack in place and remove pins. Using one strand of gold thread, backstitch the band to the fabric, stitching one block in from the edge along the top and bottom of the band.

Making Up the Bag

4 Fold the fabric right sides together and stitch the side seams about 1.3cm (½in) in from the edges, leaving a 2.5cm (1in) gap 4cm (2in) below the top edge for a channel for the cord. Press seams. Neaten raw edges and prevent fraying by over sewing them. On the top edge create a casing for the cord by turning over 2.5cm (1in) twice and stitching in place. Remove tacking and press. Use a safety pin to thread the cord through the opening in the side seam and then knot the ends together. To finish, paint fray check liquid on the cord ends.

Play Cube

This delightful soft cube will not only be fun for a child to play with but can also be used to teach them their ABC. The cube has six faces, each of which can show a different letter.

STITCH COUNT (each design)
45h x 45w
DESIGN SIZE (each design)
8.3 x 8.3cm (3¼ x 3¼in)

MATERIALS (for one cube)
✿ Six squares of 14-count Aida in pastel shades (or a single colour if you prefer), each piece 12.7 x 12.7cm (5 x 5in)
✿ Tapestry needle size 24–26
✿ DMC stranded cotton (floss) as listed in chart key
✿ Coats Ophir thread 300 gold
✿ Sewing threads to tone with Aida colours
✿ Flame-retardant (BS 5852), non-toxic, washable polyester toy filling, about 80g (3oz)

1 Prepare your fabric squares for work and mark the centre on each (see page 98). Choose six letters (or A–F) and follow the charts on pages 34–41. Stitch from the centre of the chart and centre of each fabric square.

2 Work over one block of Aida and use two strands of stranded cotton (floss) for full and three-quarter cross stitches. Use two strands for any French knots and one strand for backstitches.

Making Up the Cube

3 When the stitching is complete tack a line of stitches five Aida blocks out from the cross stitching, forming a square around each image – this will be your stitching line for assembling the cube.

4 Begin with the base square, pinning and tacking a square to each side, as shown in the diagram below (don't worry about the orientation of each side; just position them to please you). Using matching sewing thread, stitch each seam individually, starting and finishing off thread securely and keeping your seams on the stitching lines. Finger press each seam as you go. Now fold each side square upwards, sides meeting and right sides facing inwards and stitch the sides together. Pin, tack and stitch two sides of the top square in place, leaving one side open. Turn the cube through to right side and stuff with the filling. To finish, slipstitch the remaining seam closed and remove tacking.

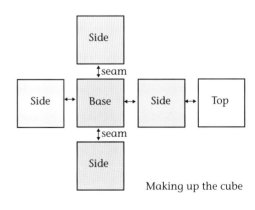

Making up the cube

Initial Notebook

For a quick but very personal gift you could stitch the initial of a friend or member of the family and mount it on to a pretty notebook. The alphabets and numbers charted on page 75 could be used to personalize the designs, to add names or messages.

STITCH COUNT
(for design shown)
45h x 45w
DESIGN SIZE
8.3 x 8.3cm (3¼ x 3¼in)

MATERIALS
✿ 12.7 x 12.7cm (5 x 5in)
   14-count white Aida
✿ Tapestry needle size 24–26
✿ DMC stranded cotton (floss)
   as listed in chart key
✿ Coats Ophir thread 300 gold
✿ 9 x 9cm (3½ x 3½in) piece
   of stiff white card
✿ Notebook, at least
   14cm (5½in) wide
✿ Double-sided adhesive tape

1 Prepare your fabric for work and mark the centre (see page 98). Follow the chart of your choice (pages 34–41) and begin stitching from the centre of the chart and centre of the fabric.

2 Work over one block of Aida and use two strands of stranded cotton (floss) for full and three-quarter cross stitches. Use two strands for any French knots and one strand for all backstitches.

3 When the embroidery is complete remove any guide lines and mount on to the white card either by lacing across the back with sewing thread or sticking in position with double-sided tape. Fix the mounted embroidery to the front of the notebook with tape. If your notebook doesn't have any embellishments, you could add some stick-on decorations.

Bearing Gifts...

The circus teddies are easy to combine to create names, signs and messages. Plan your word out on graph paper first and see page 98 for working out stitch count and finished design size before you cut your fabric and begin stitching. There are many stores that sell great ready-made frames.

Pen Pot

A pen pot makes a practical yet fun project. The finished result is a cylinder of fabric, the size of which could be changed to decorate other items, such as a birthday cake.

STITCH COUNT
45h x 45w
DESIGN SIZE
8.3 x 8.3cm (3¼ x 3¼in)
MATERIALS

✿ White 14-count Aida: width equal to the circumference of your pot plus 2.5cm (1in); height equal to three times the height of your pot

✿ Tapestry needle size 24–26

✿ DMC stranded cotton (floss) as listed in chart key

✿ Coats Ophir thread 300 gold

✿ Pen pot 9cm (3½in) high

✿ White sewing thread

✿ Narrow white bias binding, the circumference of your pot plus 2.5cm (1in)

1 Prepare your fabric for work and mark the centre (see page 98). Follow the chart of your choice (pages 34–41) and begin stitching from the centre of the chart and fabric. A large piece of Aida is used so that the excess can be folded over to conceal the back of your stitching (especially important if a transparent or mesh pot is used) and give a padded look to the finished item.

2 Work over one block of Aida and use two strands of stranded cotton (floss) for full and three-quarter cross stitches. Use two strands for any French knots and one strand for all backstitches.

3 With right sides together stitch a 1cm (⅜in) seam along the shorter edge to form a cylinder. Turn right side out. Fold an even amount of Aida up from the base and down from the top to match the pot height. With white thread, backstitch through two layers along the top and bottom one Aida block in from the edge. Turn inside out and slipstitch the bias binding over the raw edge on the lower inside edge. Turn right side out. Slip the cylinder over the pot – it has to be a slightly tight fit to give a smooth finish.

Baby's Bib

A circus bear is perfect as a quick-stitch project especially if you use a bib that already has a cross stitch insert (e.g., from DMC). On the bib mark the centre point of the area to be stitched. Begin stitching from the centre of the chart and centre of the marked area. If using a standard bib, stitch the design on to a 12.7cm (5in) square of 14-count Aida. Work over one block and use two strands of stranded cotton (floss) for full and three-quarter cross stitches and for French knots and one strand for backstitches. Press the finished embroidery. If using a standard bib, turn under the edges of the embroidery all round and stitch it into place with matching thread.

Stitch count (for design shown) 45h x 45w
Design size 8.3 x 8.3cm (3¼ x 3¼in)

A B C D

DMC stranded cotton

Cross stitch (2 strands)

▦ 208	▦ 350	⊙ 746	▦ 912	▦ 3799
− 209	▦ 437	N 777	⊙ 995	▭ 3804
▦ 210	T 606	▦ 814	H 996	△ 3843
▦ 321	\ 677	▦ 910	+ 3350	▦ 3844
V 349	▦ 738	∕ 911	∧ 3716	⌐ 3845

• blanc

▨ Coats Ophir
gold 300

Backstitch (1 strand)

—— 3799

═══ Ophir gold
300

French knots (2 strands)

⊙ Ophir gold 300

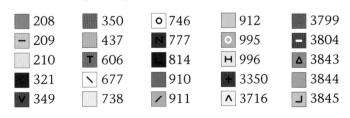

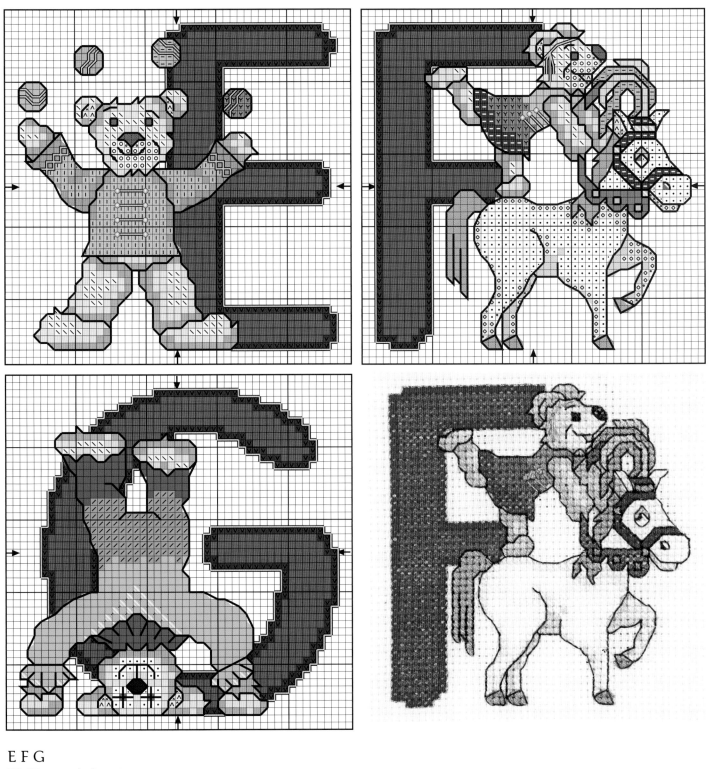

E F G
DMC stranded cotton
Cross stitch (2 strands)

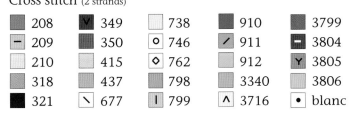

208	349	738	910	3799
209	350	746	911	3804
210	415	762	912	3805
318	437	798	3340	3806
321	677	799	3716	blanc

Coats Ophir gold 300

Backstitch (1 strand)
— 3799
Ophir gold 300

French knots (2 strands)
Ophir gold 300

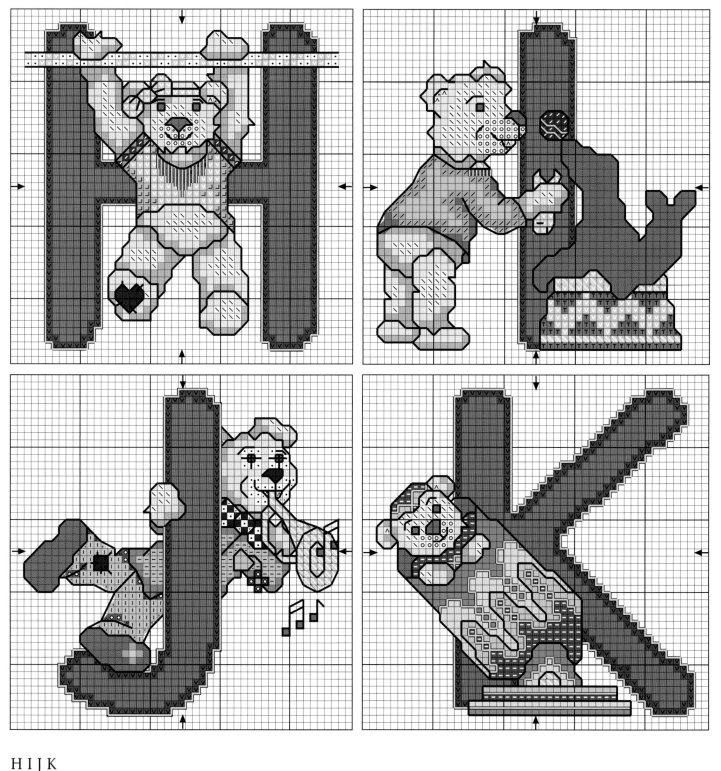

H I J K
DMC stranded cotton
Cross stitch (2 strands)

▨ 208	✓ 349	＼ 677	Ｉ 799	∧ 3716	⌐ 3845	
− 209	▨ 350	738	910	3799	∨ 3846	
210	415	○ 746	／ 911	− 3804	• blanc	
318	437	◢ 796	912	3806		
▨ 321	⊤ 606	◐ 797	3340	3844	▨ Coats Ophir gold 300	

Backstitch (1 strand)
— 3799
▭ Ophir gold 300

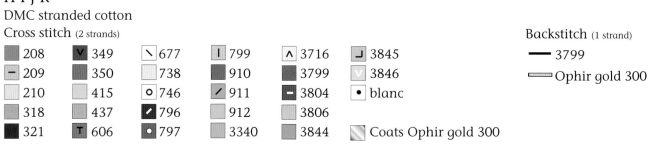

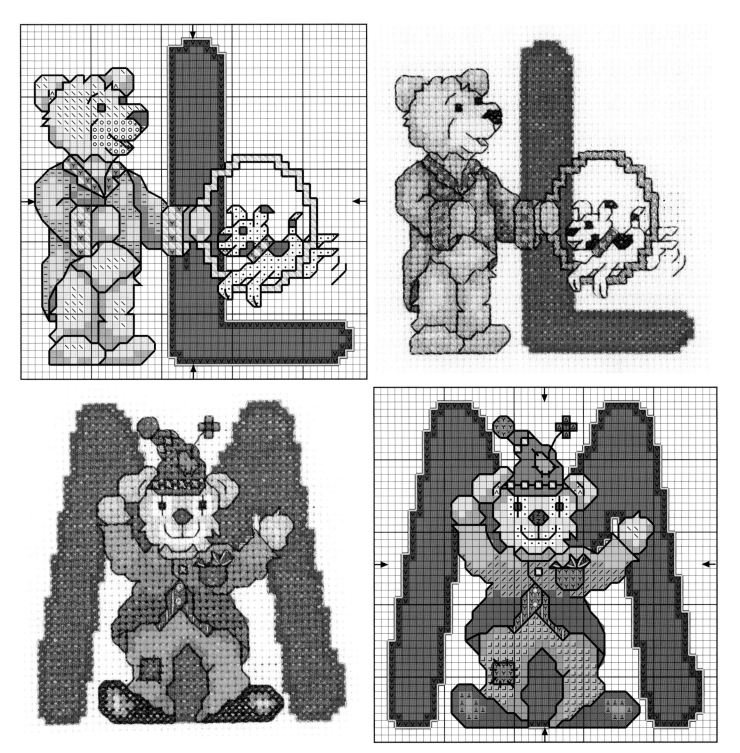

L M

DMC stranded cotton

Cross stitch (2 strands)

▨ 208	▨ 350	░ 738	▨ 3340	△ 3843
− 209	⊥ 414	○ 746	∧ 3716	▨ 3844
░ 210	▨ 437	▨ 910	▨ 3799	⌐ 3845
▨ 318	⊤ 606	∕ 911	Z 3801	• blanc
V 349	＼ 677	░ 912	⋎ 3805	▨ Coats Ophir gold 300

Backstitch (1 strand)

— 3799

═ Ophir gold 300

French knots (2 strands)

◎ Ophir gold 300

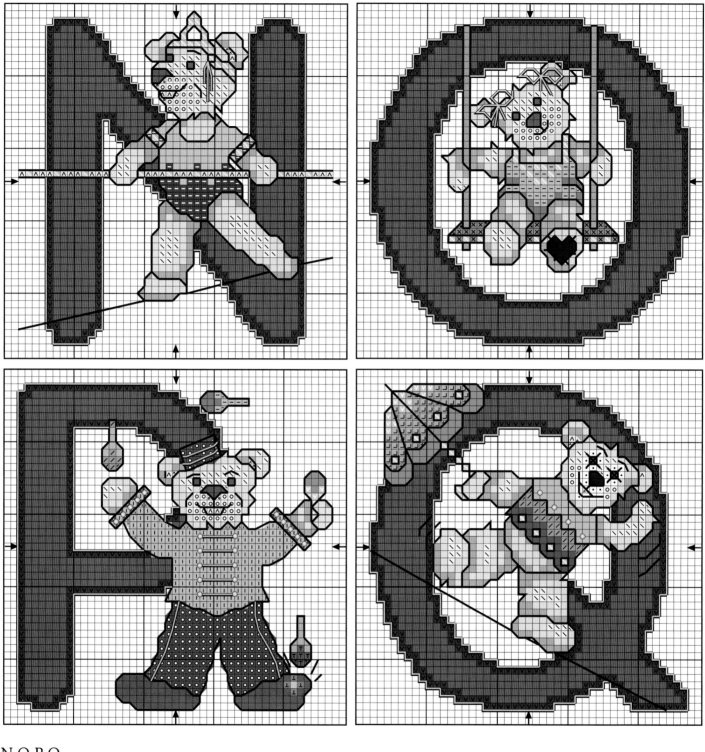

N O P Q
DMC stranded cotton
Cross stitch (2 strands)

208	350	✗ 608	❘ 799
− 209	⊥ 414	＼ 677	910
318	415	738	╱ 911
321	437	○ 746	912
⩔ 349	⊤ 606	⦿ 797	3340

⋀ 3716	⌐ 3845	
3799	⋁ 3846	
⊟ 3804	• blanc	
3806		
3844	▨ Coats Ophir gold 300	

Backstitch (1 strand)
— 3799
═══ Ophir gold 300

French knots (2 strands)
◯ Ophir gold 300

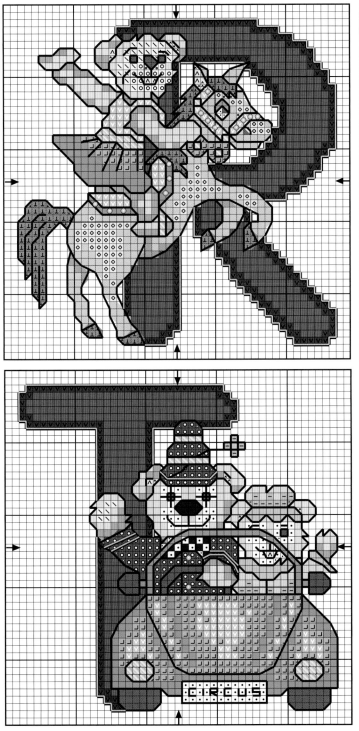

The German company, Steiff, founded by
Margarete Steiff, has been making toys since
1880. Her nephew Richard had an idea to make
a jointed toy bear standing upright after seeing
bears performing in a circus. Up until that time
bears had been made standing on all four legs.
This new idea was a huge success and in 1907
alone, Steiff produced an amazing 975,000 bears.

R S T

DMC stranded cotton

Cross stitch (2 strands)

− 209	350	738	912	⌐ 3845
210	⊥ 414	o 746	∧ 3716	3846
318	415	◇ 762	3799	• blanc
321	437	◉ 797	3806	
V 349	\ 677	/ 911	3844	▨ Coats Ophir

Backstitch (1 strand)

— 3799

▭ Ophir gold 300

French knots (2 strands)

◉ Ophir gold 300

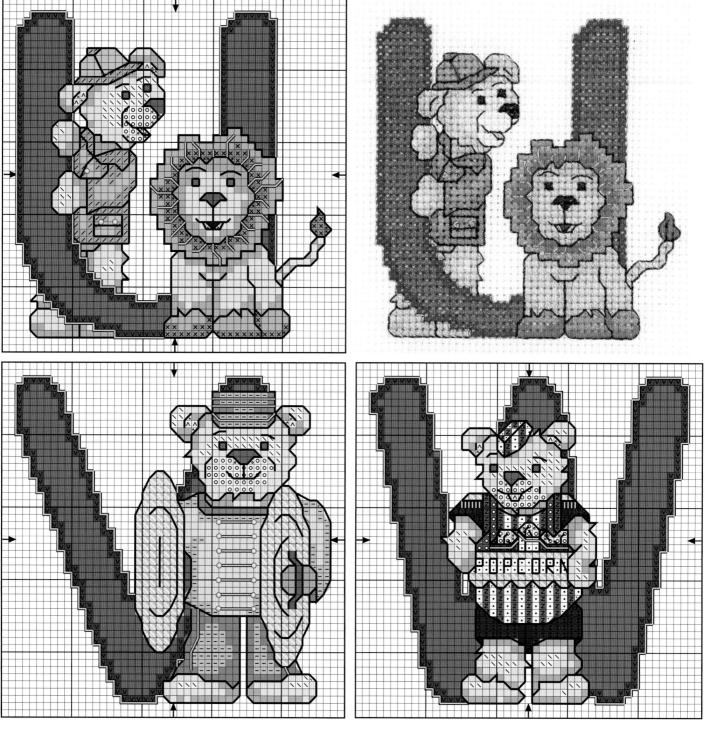

U V W

DMC stranded cotton

Cross stitch (2 strands)

■ 208	■ 350	738	3340	◢ Coats Ophir	
− 209	■ 437	○ 746	∧ 3716	gold 300	
210	✕ 608	• 797	3799		
■ 321	⊥ 666	╱ 911	Z 3801		
V 349	╲ 677	912	• blanc		

Backstitch (1 strand)

— 3799

Ophir gold
300

French knots (2 strands)

◯ Ophir gold 300

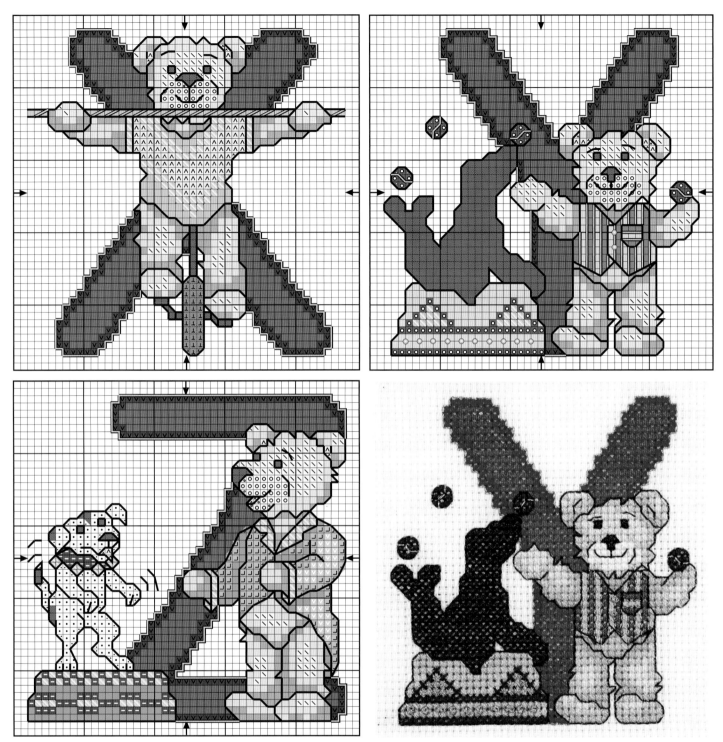

X Y Z

DMC stranded cotton

Cross stitch (2 strands)

208	437	∧ 3716	⌐ 3845
210	＼ 677	3799	3846
▼ 349	738	‒ 3804	• blanc
350	○ 746	3806	
⊥ 414	◉ 797	3844	▨ Coats Ophir gold 300

Backstitch (1 strand)

— 3799

▦ Ophir gold 300

French knots (2 strands)

◉ Ophir gold 300

Designed by Joan Elliott

Why I Love My Teddy

For so many years now teddy bears have been the childhood

symbol of affection and love – be it a new-found friend for your

darling little one or an old chum, torn and tattered from those many years of

hugs and kisses. Teddies are always at the ready to lend an ear for our most important

secrets, or give us much-needed comfort on a dark and stormy night.

There must be hundreds of reasons to love teddies and the six endearing

sentiments on this wall hanging express some loving thoughts about these charming

companions. Cuddle up with a project that will bring a smile to any teddy bear fan.

This hanging, with its cheerful pastel colours, will fit perfectly in any child's room

(or yours!). You could stitch it just as it is or choose one of the six bears to create

many smaller projects – see suggestions throughout the chapter. There are also many

smaller but equally sweet motifs that could be used for quick-stitch cards and gift

tags. The alphabets and numbers charted on page 75 could be used to create names

and messages.

The sentiments on this lovely wall hanging will always raise a smile and, like a teddy, will never grow old. So, why do I love my teddy? – because he loves me!

Why I Love My Teddy Wall Hanging

This charming wall hanging design is great fun to stitch. Instead of making the design up as a hanging, you could frame it as a picture. See overleaf for more ideas on how to use the design. It is a large design so do ensure that you use a big enough piece of fabric and make sure you begin stitching from the centre of the fabric.

STITCH COUNT
321h x 111w

DESIGN SIZE
58.2 x 20.3cm (23 x 8in)

MATERIALS

❀ 71 x 33cm (28 x 13in) Fiddler's Light 14-count Aida

❀ Tapestry needle size 24

❀ DMC stranded cotton (floss) as listed in chart key

❀ 0.25m (¼yd) lightweight iron-on interfacing

❀ 0.5m (½yd) background print fabric

❀ 0.5m (½yd) fusible fleece

❀ 0.25m (¼yd) fusible web

❀ 1.8m (2yd) decorative trim to tone with embroidery

❀ Four decorative buttons

❀ Permanent fabric glue

❀ 33cm (13in) length of dowel painted to tone with the embroidery

It has been estimated that 40% of adults still own their childhood teddy bear.

1 Prepare for work, referring to page 98 if necessary. Mark the centre of the fabric and centre of the chart on pages 48–51. Mount your fabric in an embroidery frame if you wish.

2 Start stitching from the centre of the chart and the centre of the piece of fabric, using two strands of stranded cotton (floss) for full and three-quarter cross stitches. Work all French knots using two strands wound once around the needle. Following the chart colours, use one strand for backstitches and any long stitches.

3 Once all the stitching is complete make up as a wall hanging as follows. Cut a piece of iron-on interfacing 2.5cm (1in) larger than the finished embroidery all around. With the wrong side of your work facing, centre the interfacing and fuse it to the embroidery. Trim the embroidery seven rows beyond the design.

4 Now cut two 71.2 x 33cm (28 x 13in) pieces of background fabric plus three 15 x 10cm (6 x 4in) pieces for hanging tabs. Cut a 71.2 x 33cm (28 x 13in) piece of fusible fleece and fuse this to the wrong side of one of the fabric pieces following the manufacturer's instructions.

5 To make the tabs, fold each piece of 15 x 10cm (6 x 4in) fabric in half lengthwise, right sides together. Sew a 1.3cm (½in) seam down the length and across one short end. Trim the seam, turn right side out and press. Place the two pieces of background fabric with right sides facing and pin the tabs between the layers, placing them evenly across the top of the hanging with sewn ends pointing towards the centre and with raw edges matching. Stitch a 1.3cm (½in) seam all around leaving a gap at the bottom for turning. Turn right side out and press. Slipstitch the gap closed.

6 Cut a piece of fusible web to the same size as the prepared embroidery. On the piece of fabric backed with fleece, centre the embroidery with the fusible web carefully placed behind it. Fuse according to the manufacturer's instructions. Glue the length of decorative trim carefully to the raw edge of the embroidery, starting and ending at centre bottom, sewing on one of the decorative buttons where the ends meet.

7 Bring the loose ends of the tabs to the front and attach to the hanging by sewing on three decorative buttons. Finally, insert the dowel through the tabs, ready to hang the wall hanging.

The teddy bear gets its name from US President Theodore 'Teddy' Roosevelt. In 1902 he refused to shoot a bear cub while out hunting, prompting toy maker, Morris Mitchum, to ask if he could name a new toy after the President – and so 'Teddy's Bear' was born.

Bearing Gifts...

This wall hanging design is full of charming motifs that you could use for a wide range of gifts and cards. Some of the tiny motifs would also be perfect for gift tags.

This happy teddy is certainly full of the joys of life and would be perfect for a card celebrating a special occasion, perhaps for someone who has just passed their driving test, or following examination success. A torn-up L plate is easy to create with some card and a red felt-tip pen.

The hot-water bottle project on page 88 is so charming you are sure to want to use it to display other cross stitch designs, such as this ready-for-bed teddy. Using a print fleece would be fun.

Even the smaller motifs on this versatile wall hanging can be used to create original gifts. The two little teddies from the top of the design could be stitched on Aida or linen band to create a band for a birthday cake.

This sweet teddy is overflowing with love, so why not use him to adorn a special gift to someone you love? Back the embroidery with iron-on interfacing, trim to shape and use double-sided tape to fix the patch to a box of chocolates or other treats and edge it with a pretty braid – perfect for Valentine's Day.

A little bird told me it's a special day...

HAPPY BIRTHDAY!!

Make a delightful birthday card using this teddy and his friends, creating a message on the card with stick-on letters or a decorative pen. Craft shops usually have self-adhesive ribbon, lace and broderie anglaise, which would add a pretty finishing touch to the card.

Why not stitch one of the teddies on some beautiful hand-dyed variegated fabric? The painting teddy would look great on the front of a sketch pad. Glue the patch to the pad and edge with some twisted braid.

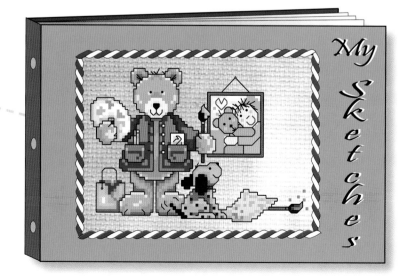

My Sketches

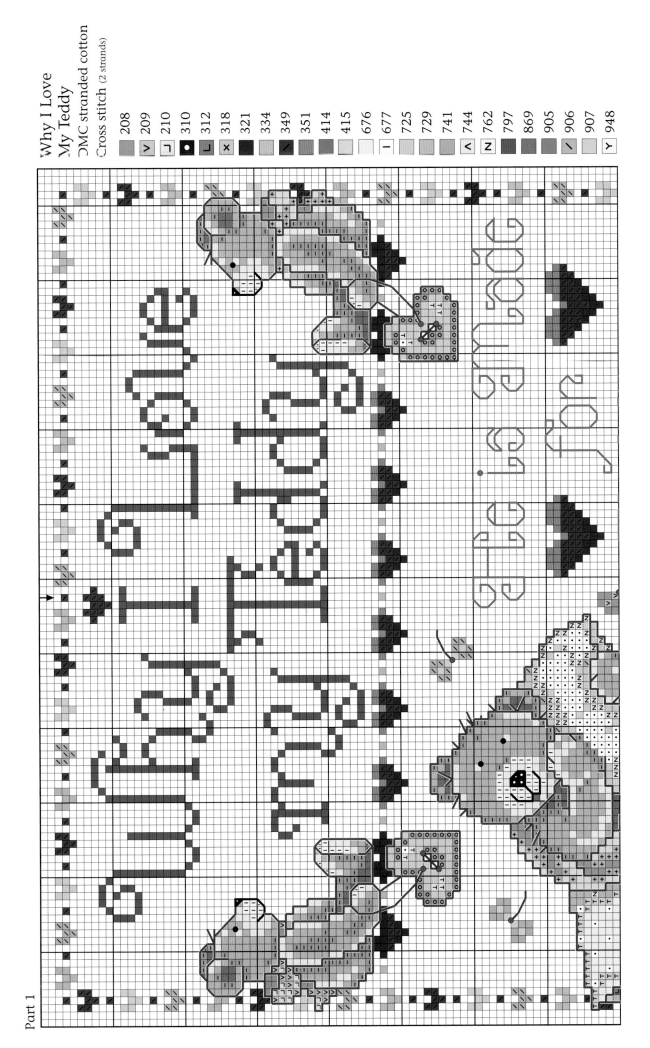

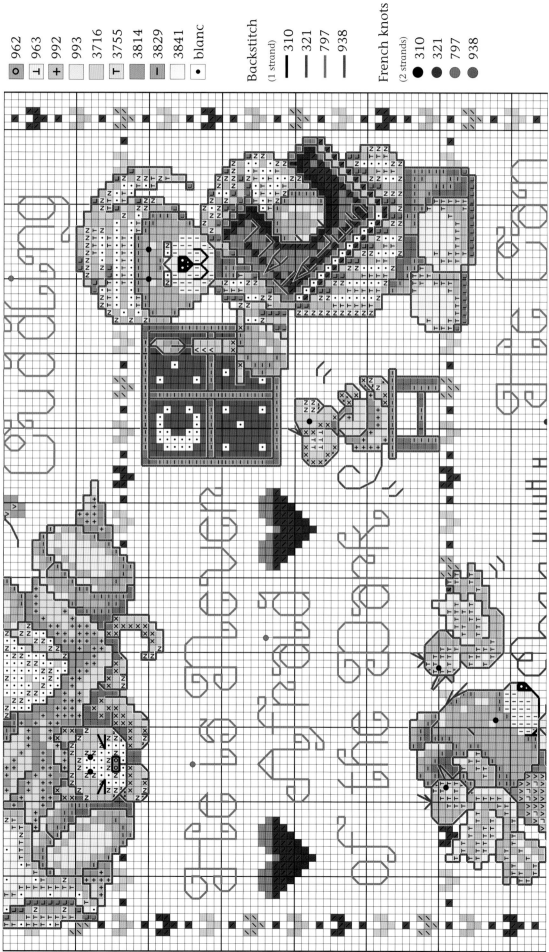

Part 2

49

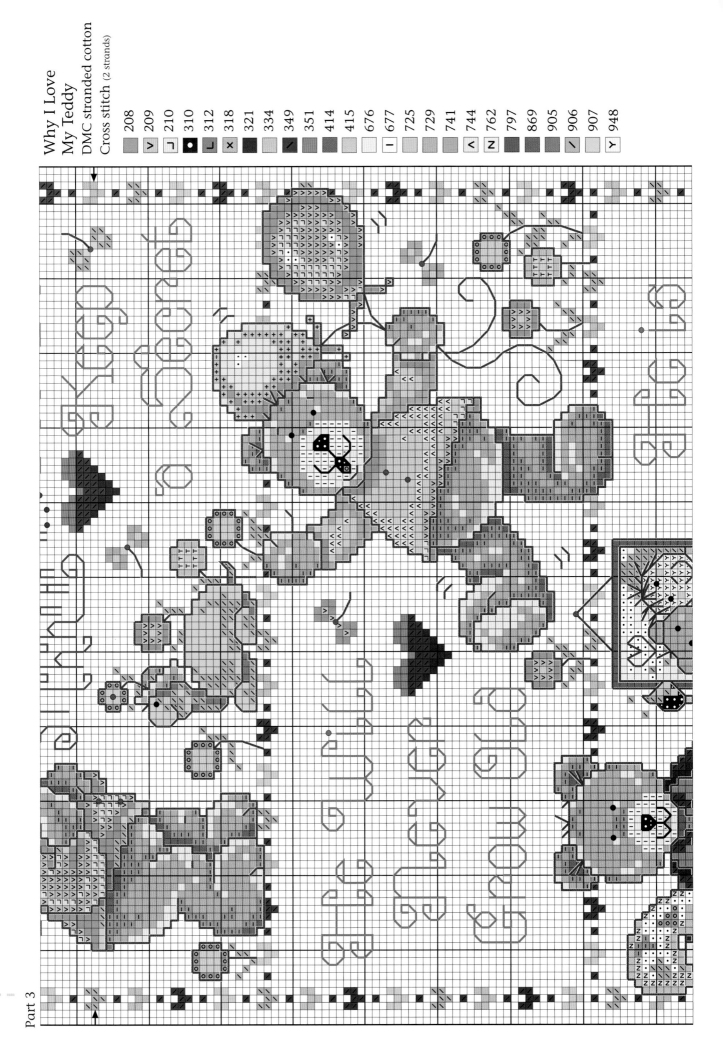

208
209
210
310
312
318
321
334
349
351
414
415
676
677
725
729
741
744
762
797
869
905
906
907
948

962
963
992
993
3716
3755
3814
3829
3841
blanc

Backstitch
(1 strand)
310
321
797
938

French knots
(2 strands)
310
321
797
938

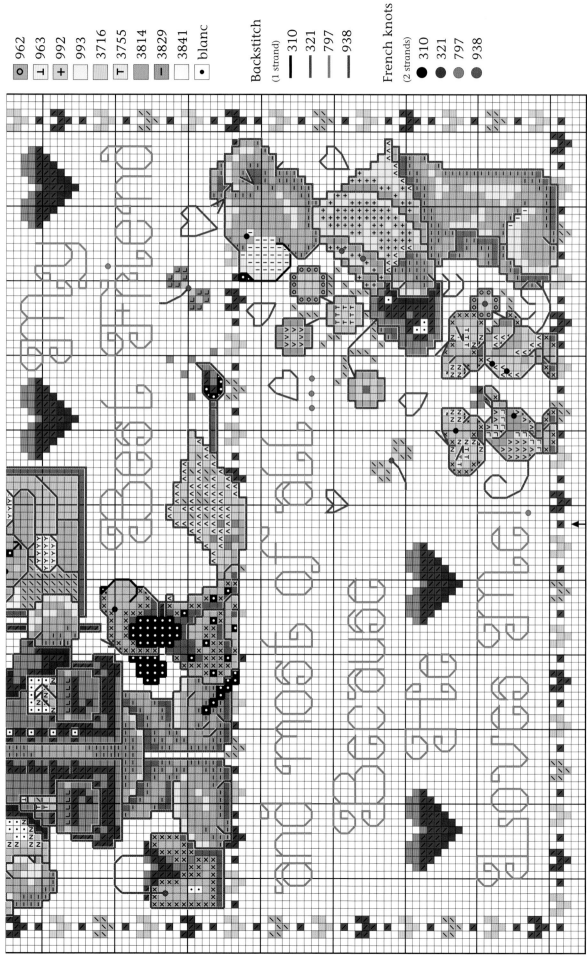

Designed by Joanne Sanderson

Bears in the Kitchen

Most of the teddy bears we are familiar with adore their food –

whether it's Winnie the Pooh and his overflowing jars of sticky honey

or Paddington Bear and his dripping marmalade sandwiches, like most

of us, they love sweet things. The kitchen teddies in this chapter are doing what

bears do best – preparing, eating and enjoying their food, especially sweet treats.

Use these great designs to bring an extra splash of fun and colour to the room you

probably spend most of your time in. Bears seldom need any encouragement to eat

and a handy apron will show that you, too, mean business in the kitchen. The Ready,

Steady, Cook design shown opposite can be made into a useful pocket or be sewn

to the apron as a decorative patch. The Teddy's Treats design looks great on the cookie

jar on page 55 but could also be used on a recipe book cover. Taking life one cookie

at a time seems wise advice and three plump teddies are ideal for practical coasters

(see page 56). A hand towel on page 57, decorated with a quick and easy

embroidered band, completes the set.

The versatile designs in this chapter are perfect for creating attractive items for the kitchen. The many small motifs in the apron design shown opposite would be ideal for coasters, key rings or fridge magnets.

Ready, Teddy, Cook Apron

This design shows cook busy in the kitchen making scrumptious things. You could use this design on an apron or frame it as a picture to brighten a kitchen wall. The instructions describe how to make an apron from a tea towel but you could use a ready-made apron.

STITCH COUNT
100h x 130w
DESIGN SIZE
18.2 x 23.6cm (7⅛ x 9¼in)

MATERIALS

❀ 30.5 x 35.5cm (12 x 14in) 14-count cream Aida

❀ Tapestry needle size 24–26

❀ DMC stranded cotton (floss) as listed in chart key

❀ Large, thick tea towel or piece of fabric 76 x 56cm (30 x 22in)

❀ Fabric for backing pocket

❀ Ribbon tape for ties, three pieces each 60cm (24in)

❀ Sewing thread to match Aida and apron

❀ Decorative braid (optional), approx 1.5m (1½yd), cut into three equal lengths

1 Prepare your fabric for work and mark the centre (see page 98). Follow the chart on pages 58–59 and begin stitching from the centre of the chart and centre of the fabric, working over one Aida block.

2 Use two strands of stranded cotton (floss) for full and three-quarter cross stitches. Work French knots using two strands wound once around the needle. Use one strand for light and dark grey backstitches and two strands for white backstitches.

3 Prepare the patch by trimming the Aida to within 3.8cm (1½in) of the embroidery all round. Cut a piece of backing fabric the same size. Pin the pieces right sides together and using matching sewing thread sew around all sides, leaving a gap at the bottom for turning through. Clip corners to reduce bulk, turn through to right side, turn out the corners and press seams.

Making the apron

4 Take your tea towel or fabric rectangle and following Fig 1 fold the top corners over to the back. Leaving about 2.5cm (1in) of fabric for a seam allowance, cut off the spare fabric and hem the raw edges. Take a length of ribbon tape and sew it to the inside neck of the apron, making sure the loop will fit over your head. Use the other two lengths of tape as waist ties, attaching one to each side of the apron (Fig 2).

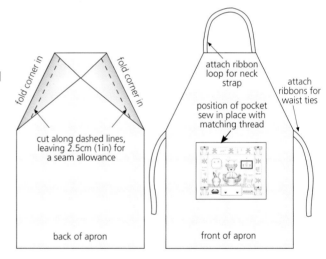

Fig 1 Creating the apron shape

Fig 2 Attaching the pocket and ties

5 Pin the pocket in place on the apron front and using matching thread attach it with small running stitches around the sides and bottom, leaving the top open. If using the embroidery as a patch, sew it to the apron around all sides. Edge the pocket with braid, sewing it in place with matching thread. If desired, add decorative stitches to the ric-rac using six strands of stranded cotton in a contrasting colour. To finish, press the apron and pocket.

Cookie Bear Jar

This kitchen teddy design can be used to decorate all sorts of items – a cookie jar as shown here or on the lid of a biscuit tin or any container filled with treats.

STITCH COUNT
60h x 60w

DESIGN SIZE
10.8 x 10.8cm (4¼ x 4¼in)

MATERIALS

❀ 20.3 x 20.3cm (8 x 8in)
  14-count white Aida

❀ Tapestry needle size 24–26

❀ DMC stranded cotton (floss)
  as listed in chart key

❀ Suitable jar or tin

❀ 20.3 x 20.3cm (8 x 8in)
  iron-on interfacing

❀ Craft glue or double-sided
  adhesive tape

1 Prepare your fabric for work and mark the centre (see page 98). Follow the chart on page 61 and begin stitching from the centre of the chart and centre of the fabric, working over one Aida block.

2 Use two strands of stranded cotton (floss) for full and three-quarter cross stitches. Work all French knots using two strands wound once around the needle. Use one strand for backstitches.

3 When all stitching is complete, press the fabric (see page 99) and iron the interfacing on to the back (see page 101). Trim the fabric so the finished stitching lies centrally and stick it to the jar with craft glue or double-sided tape. Alternatively, sew ribbon to either side of the patch and tie it around the jar.

Bearing Gifts...

The Teddy's Treats design would also make a wonderful patch for a recipe book cover. Back the finished embroidery with iron-on interfacing, trim to size and use double-sided adhesive tape to fix it to your recipe book. Protect the edges of the patch with decorative braid glued into place and finish with some decorative buttons.

Hungry Bear Coasters

Three charming designs can be used to make a useful set of coasters – perfect for coffee mornings with friends. You could also use these little bears to adorn table mats.

STITCH COUNT (each design)
40h x 40w

DESIGN SIZE
7.2 x 7.2cm (2⅞ x 2⅞in)

MATERIALS (for each coaster)
✿ 15.2 x 15.2cm (6 x 6in) 14-count white Aida
✿ Tapestry needle size 24–26
✿ DMC stranded cotton (floss) as listed in chart key
✿ Acrylic coaster 7.6cm (3in) square (from Framecraft – see Suppliers)
✿ 15.2 x 15.2cm (6 x 6in) square of iron-on interfacing

1 Prepare your fabric for work and mark the centre (see page 98). Follow the chart on page 60 and begin stitching from the centre of the chart and the centre of the fabric, working over one Aida block.

2 Use two strands of stranded cotton (floss) for full and three-quarter cross stitches. Work all French knots using two strands wound once around the needle. Use one strand for backstitches.

3 When all stitching is complete, press the fabric (see page 99) and iron the interfacing on to the back of the fabric (see page 101). Trim the fabric so that the finished stitching lies centrally within the coaster aperture and then assemble the coaster following the manufacturer's instructions.

Teddy bears are popular worldwide, although the word for 'bear' varies of course. Here are some examples.

Welsh – arwedda	Finnish – kannattaa
Icelandic – bjorn	Romanian – urs
Italian – orso	Danish – bamsen

Cookie Bear Towel

The cutest little teddies make a quick and easy adornment for a towel. Simply repeat the charted design as often as necessary to create a band for a towel. You could also stitch a band to edge a small tablecloth.

STITCH COUNT
(for one repeat)
22h x 57w
DESIGN SIZE
3.8 x 10.2cm (1½ x 4in)
MATERIALS
- 5cm (2in) wide 14-count white Aida band, the length of towel plus 5cm (2in)
- Tapestry needle size 24–26
- DMC stranded cotton (floss) as listed in chart key
- Hand towel
- Matching sewing thread

1 Prepare your fabric for work and follow the chart on page 61. Begin stitching 2.5cm (1in) in from the left-hand edge of the band and work over one Aida block.

2 Use three strands of stranded cotton (floss) for full and three-quarter cross stitches. Work French knots using two strands wound once around the needle. Use one strand for dark grey backstitches and two strands for white backstitches. Repeat the design, as shown on the chart, as often as necessary.

3 When all stitching is complete, press the band (see page 99). Attach the band to the towel by hand or machine stitching, using white sewing thread. Turn each end of the band under neatly before stitching securely in place.

Bearing Gifts...

The little cookie bears could be used to make a useful coat rack for a child's room. Stitch the red hearts further up the design to allow room for some coat hooks or wooden knobs. Back the stitching with iron-on interfacing and glue it to a rectangle of pine or other wood. Screw the hooks or knobs directly into the fabric and through into the wood and then screw the rack to the wall.

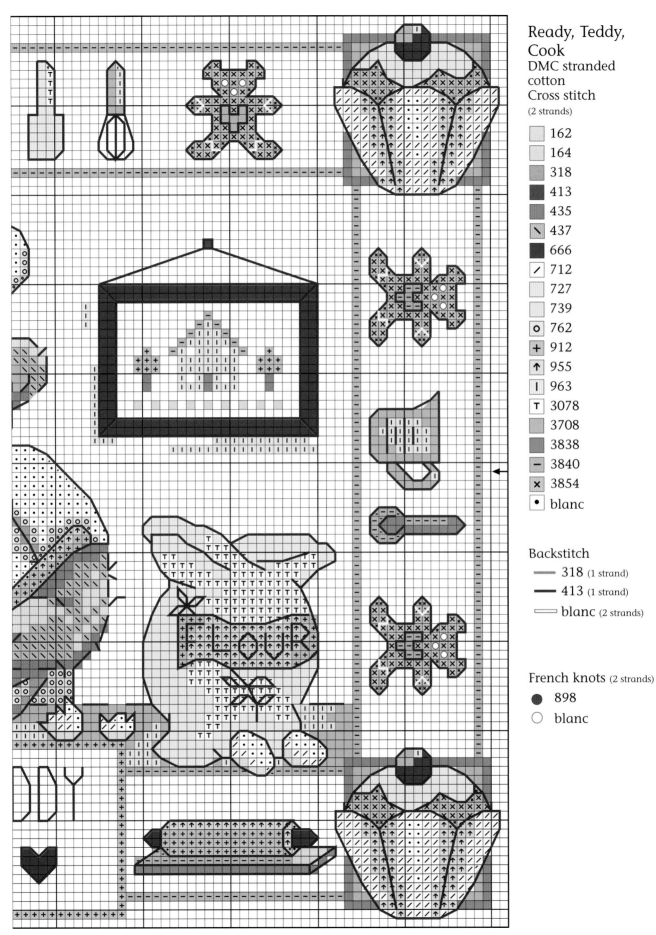

Ready, Teddy, Cook

DMC stranded cotton
Cross stitch
(2 strands)

	162
	164
	318
	413
	435
\	437
	666
/	712
	727
	739
o	762
+	912
↑	955
I	963
T	3078
	3708
	3838
−	3840
×	3854
•	blanc

Backstitch

— 318 (1 strand)
— 413 (1 strand)
— blanc (2 strands)

French knots (2 strands)

● 898
○ blanc

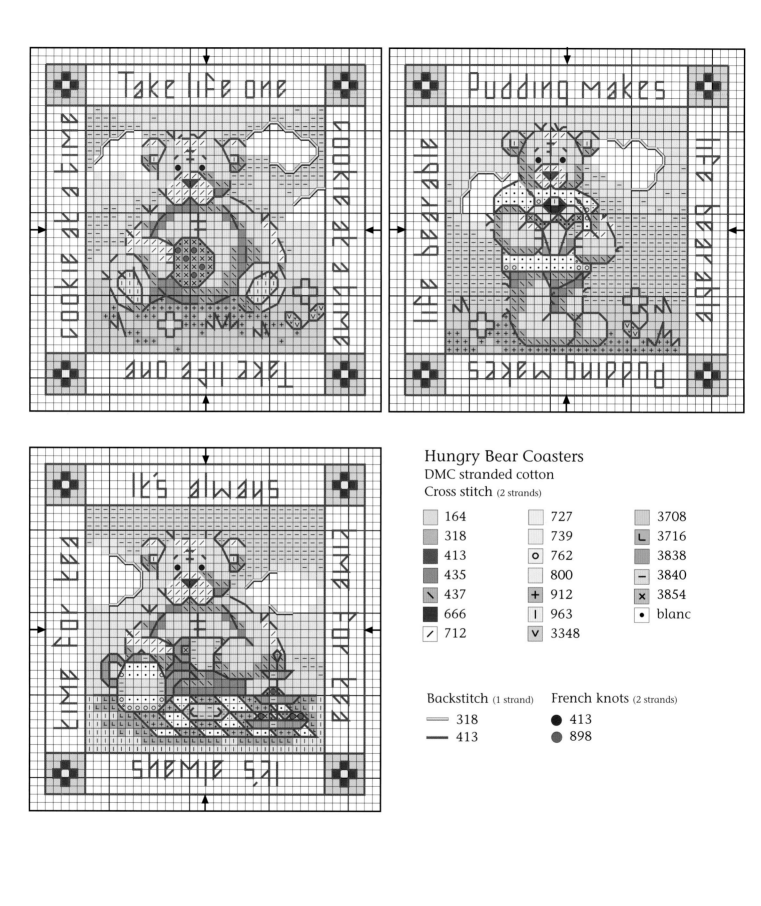

Hungry Bear Coasters
DMC stranded cotton
Cross stitch (2 strands)

164	727	3708
318	739	L 3716
413	o 762	3838
435	800	— 3840
\ 437	+ 912	× 3854
666	I 963	• blanc
/ 712	v 3348	

Backstitch (1 strand)   **French knots** (2 strands)
— 318   ● 413
— 413   ● 898

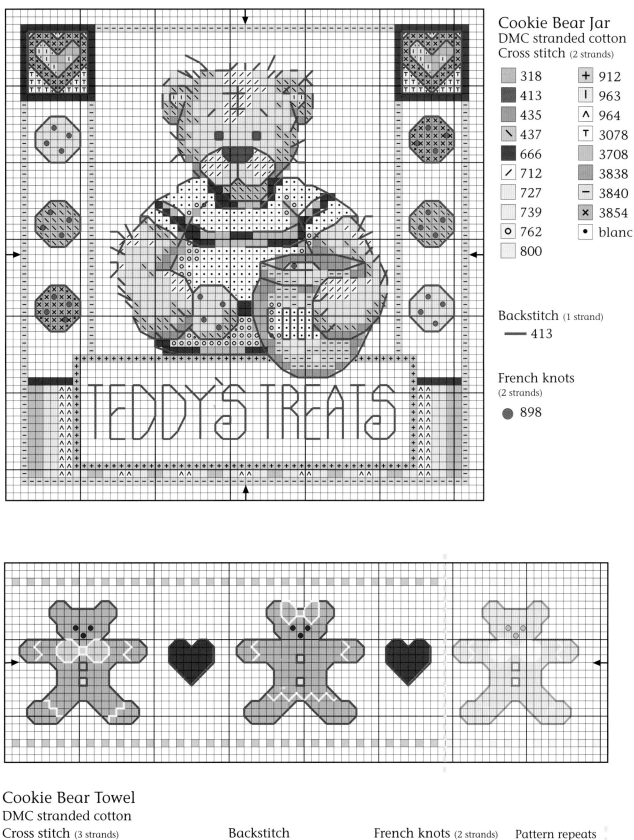

Cookie Bear Jar
DMC stranded cotton
Cross stitch (2 strands)

▨	318	+	912
▨	413	I	963
▨	435	∧	964
\	437	T	3078
▨	666	▨	3708
/	712	▨	3838
▨	727	−	3840
▨	739	✕	3854
○	762	•	blanc
▨	800		

Backstitch (1 strand)
—— 413

French knots
(2 strands)
● 898

Cookie Bear Towel
DMC stranded cotton
Cross stitch (3 strands)

▨	666	▨	912	▨	3840
▨	727	▨	3708	▨	3854

Backstitch
 —— 413 (1 strand)
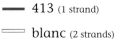 ══ blanc (2 strands)

French knots (2 strands)
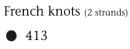 ● 413

Pattern repeats
from the blue
dashed line

Best Friends, Teddy and Me

Designed by Joanne Sanderson

Teddy bears and children must be the perfect combination and what small

baby doesn't have at least one teddy to snuggle in times of need? Perhaps that's

why we love teddies so much; they seem to embody all the endearing qualities

of young children – soft and cuddly, loyal and loving. For the very young, the world

must seem full of very large and very noisy people, so what a comfort a small, quiet

teddy bear must be.

The sweet little child in this lovely picture is in the peaceful Land of Nod, with his

best friend tucked up warm beside him. This picture, with its charming sentiment,

is perfect for a nursery, celebrating as it does that very special relationship between

a child and their teddy. There are also two delightful, hand-crafted card designs

to welcome a new baby. These designs have the touches of blue and pink that we

traditionally associate with little boys and girls but the colours are easily changed.

The chapter has lots of suggestions for other ways to use the designs.

*Teddy bears are the ultimate comforters and little ones
are swiftly off to Dreamland with their teddy bear close by.
The delicate pastels of this design will suit any décor.*

Best Friends Picture

Ten little fingers, ten little toes, two padded paws and a cute button nose – what a charming design this is. It would also make a lovely cover for an album holding precious memories of a baby's first year.

STITCH COUNT
98h x 128w
DESIGN SIZE
17.8 x 23.2cm (7 x 9⅛in)

MATERIALS
❀ White 14-count Aida
   33 x 38cm (13 x 15in)
❀ Tapestry needle size 24
❀ DMC stranded cotton (floss)
   as listed in the chart key
❀ Suitable picture frame

1 Prepare your fabric for work and mark the centre (see page 98). Follow the chart on pages 68–69 and begin stitching from the centre of the chart and centre of the fabric.

2 Work over one block of Aida and use two strands of stranded cotton (floss) for full and three-quarter cross stitches. Use two strands for the 772 half cross stitch. Use one strand for backstitch.

3 When the embroidery is complete remove any guide lines, press the work (see page 99) and then frame as desired (see page 101) or make up in some other way of your choice.

'If you go out in the woods today, you're sure of a big surprise. If you go out in the woods today, you'd better go in disguise...' Many people know these words are the beginning of one of the earliest songs about teddy bears. 'Teddy Bears' Picnic' was written by Irish songwriter Jimmy Kennedy in 1933. The jaunty music was taken from the 'Teddy Bear Two-step' written by American composer John Bratton in 1907.

The two cards shown here and opposite are perfect to celebrate a new arrival. You could also use the designs for a first birthday by changing or omitting the wording. Some alphabets and numerals are charted on page 75.

Welcome Baby Cards

Two lovely designs are perfect to welcome a new baby into the world. The teddy designs would also make sweet little pictures for the nursery or could be stitched as patches to decorate baby clothes.

STITCH COUNTS
Baby Girl 55h x 35w
Baby Boy 57h x 39w
DESIGN SIZES
Baby Girl 10.2 x 6.3cm
(4 x 2½in)
Baby Boy 10.2 x 7cm
(4 x 2¾in)

MATERIALS
✿ White 14-count Aida
20.3 x 17.8cm (8 x 7in)
✿ Tapestry needle size 24
✿ DMC stranded cotton (floss)
as listed in the chart key
✿ Iron-on interfacing
20.3 x 17.8cm (8 x 7in)
✿ Double-fold aperture card
for boy design or single-fold
card for girl design
✿ Craft glue and
double-sided tape
✿ Patterned paper
✿ Ribbon and embellishments

1 Prepare your fabric for work and mark the centre (see page 98). Follow the charts overleaf and begin stitching from the centre of the chart and fabric.

2 Work over one block of Aida and use two strands of stranded cotton (floss) for full and three-quarter cross stitches. Use two strands for French knots and then one strand for backstitch. When the embroidery is complete remove any guide lines, press the work (see page 99) and fuse iron-on interfacing to the back of the embroidery (see page 101). Trim the fabric so that the embroidery lies centrally.

3 To finish the boy card, cover the front of the card with patterned paper and trim the paper to the edge of the aperture. Mount the embroidery into the card as described on page 101 and add embellishments as desired.

To finish the girl card, glue patterned paper over the front of the card. Glue or tape the embroidered patch on to the front of the card and then embellish.

Many television programmes and films have been made featuring teddy bears. The first animated teddy-bear cartoon was made in 1909 in the USA and was called 'Little Johnny and the Teddy Bears'.

Baby Girl Card
DMC stranded cotton
Cross stitch
(2 strands)

	437
	453
	645
v	647
\	739
−	818
•	844
	962
o	3716
•	blanc

Backstitch (1 strand)

— 844

French knots (2 strands)

● 844

Bearing Gifts...

This design would look gorgeous sewn to the front of a sweet little dress or on a sun hat. For a design in a smaller finished size, work it on 16-count or 18-count Aida instead of 14-count. For a different look you could omit the words and change the three pink colours to lilacs. Back the embroidery with iron-on interfacing, sew it to the dress and edge the embroidered patch with pretty braid.

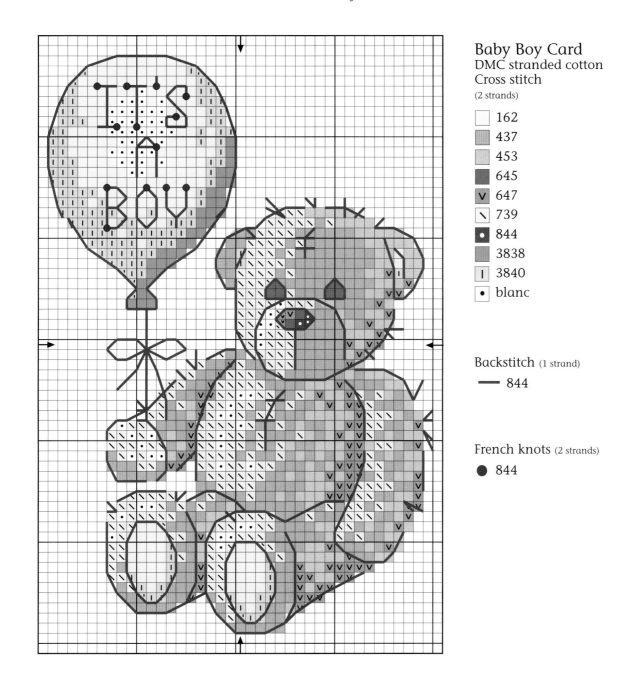

Baby Boy Card
DMC stranded cotton
Cross stitch
(2 strands)

☐	162
▦	437
▨	453
▦	645
∨	647
⟍	739
◉	844
▦	3838
I	3840
•	blanc

Backstitch (1 strand)
—— 844

French knots (2 strands)
● 844

Bearing Gifts...

This darling little teddy can be used for many projects, such as the bib shown here. If you require the design to be a smaller finished size, work it on 16-count or 18-count Aida instead of 14-count. You could change the words in the balloon to a child's name and replace the three blue colours with greens or yellows. Back the embroidery with iron-on interfacing, sew it to the bib and edge the patch with some bright braid. Bibs are available with a cross stitch insert, ready for stitching – see Suppliers on page 104.

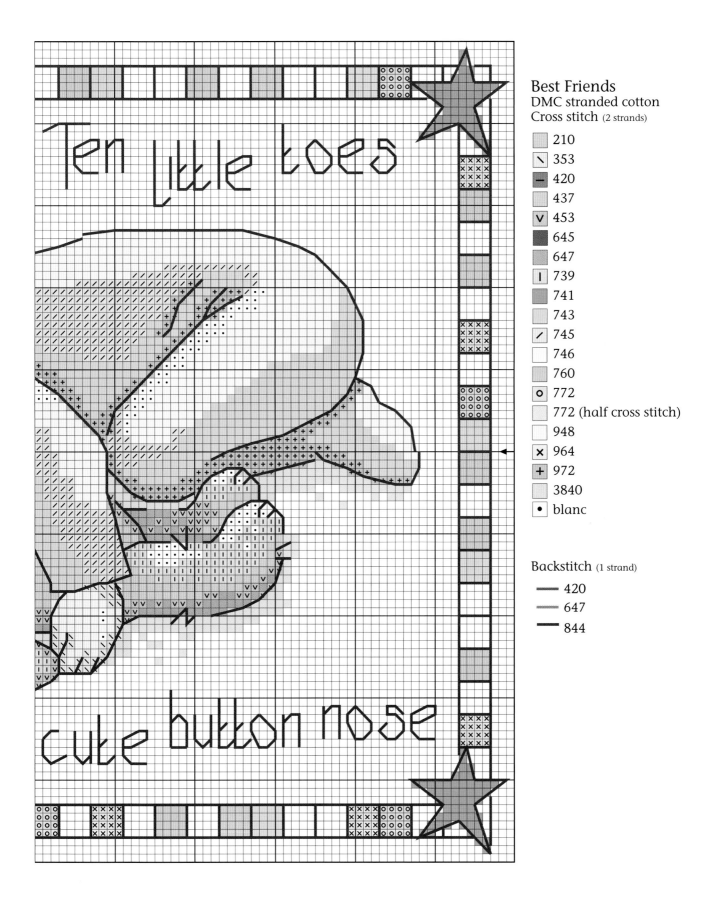

Best Friends
DMC stranded cotton
Cross stitch (2 strands)

	210
◣	353
−	420
	437
V	453
	645
	647
I	739
	741
	743
◢	745
	746
	760
○	772
	772 (half cross stitch)
	948
×	964
+	972
	3840
•	blanc

Backstitch (1 strand)

—	420
—	647
—	844

Calendar Teddies

Teddy bears have a place in our hearts every month of the year and this cheerful collection of teddies has gathered to help you celebrate with friends and family throughout the whole year.

Brighten the New Year with balloons and streamers or send heartfelt love on Valentine's Day. Spread the luck of the Irish with shamrocks galore and laugh away those April showers under a bright red umbrella. Dance around the maypole with pretty spring flowers and welcome summer with a brimming bowl of fresh strawberries. Celebrate the birth of a nation or take in the warmth of the summer sun by the sea. As the children make ready for school to begin, send some encouragement with a school house bear. A sweet teddy bear pumpkin is just the ticket for your favourite little goblin. Round out your year in a blaze of autumn leaves topped off with a teddy and snowman ready for Christmas. The designs can also be used for many other projects – see overleaf and page 74 for ideas.

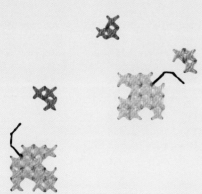

This collection of colourful cards is so versatile that you are sure to find many uses for the delightful teddy designs, not just for seasonal events but for birthday and greetings cards. See overleaf for the other six cards.

Calendar Ted Cards

These delightful teddies celebrate the year in colourful style. They are fun to stitch and are bound to bring a smile to the face of the recipient. Giving them for birthdays is only the start as there are many other ways you could use the designs. For example, the September teddy could be used on a book bag for a child just starting school. The August teddy could be stitched as a patch and sewn to a bright sun hat. On page 75 you will find alphabets and numerals charted, which can be used to create messages and personalize the designs.

STITCH COUNT (each card)
54h x 34w
DESIGN SIZE
9.8 x 6.2cm (4 x 2½in)

MATERIALS (for each card)
✿ 23 x 19cm (9 x 7½in) white 14-count Aida
✿ Tapestry needle size 24
✿ DMC stranded cotton (floss) as listed in chart key
✿ Kreinik #4 braid 028 citron
✿ Double-fold card mount (see Suppliers)

1 Prepare for work, referring to page 98 if necessary. Mark the centre of the fabric and centre of the chart (charts on pages 76–81). Mount your fabric in an embroidery frame if you wish.

2 Start stitching from the centre of the chart and fabric. Use one strand for all Kreinik thread cross stitches. Use two strands of stranded cotton (floss) for all other full and three-quarter cross stitches. Work all French knots using two strands wound once around the needle. Following the chart colours, use one strand for backstitches.

3 Once all the stitching is complete, mount your embroidery in a suitable card (see page 101). Embellish the card mount as desired. The twelve cards in this collection have been made just that bit more special by having a length of ribbon, chosen to tone with the design, tied around the card spine with a simple knot.

Monthly Flowers and Gemstones

Certain flowers and gemstones are associated with specific months and you could use these for ideas on how to embellish your Calendar Teddies cards and gifts. For example, for a February birthday choose an amethyst coloured card mount and embellish with violet flower toppers. For a June card, cover a single-fold card with rose-patterned paper and edge the embroidery with little pearls (see example below).

	Flower	Gemstone
January	❀ Carnation or Snowdrop	◆ Garnet
February	❀ Violet, Primrose or Iris	◆ Amethyst
March	❀ Daffodil	◆ Aquamarine
April	❀ Daisy or Sweet Pea	◆ Diamond
May	❀ Lily-of-the-Valley	◆ Emerald
June	❀ Rose or Honeysuckle	◆ Moonstone or Pearls
July	❀ Larkspur or Sunflower	◆ Ruby
August	❀ Poppy or Gladiola	◆ Peridot
September	❀ Aster or Morning Glory	◆ Sapphire
October	❀ Cosmos or Snapdragon	◆ Opal or Tourmaline
November	❀ Chrysanthemum	◆ Topaz or Citrine
December	❀ Holly or Orchid	◆ Turquoise or Blue Topaz

Bearing Gifts...

These teddy designs can be used as charted for a wide range of fun projects or you could stitch just the teddy and use the smaller motif for gift ideas. Some suggestions are shown here.

Let people know where you are with a handy door sign. Back the stitching with double-sided iron-on adhesive and fuse it to a rectangle of patterned fabric. Embellish the edge with decorative stitching. Fix the fabric over thick card, turn the edges to the back and glue. Add a stick-on scroll for writing your message. Make a raffia bow and fix to the back for hanging.

Make a pincushion by stitching just the February teddy on a pastel-coloured Aida or linen. Trim it to size and cut backing fabric to match. Sew the two pieces right sides together, leaving a gap. Turn through, stuff with stuffing, close the gap and add decorative braid all around the edge. Finish with a tassel and decorative button.

The teddy and snowman from the December design would make a lovely Christmas decoration. Stitch on dark blue Aida and back with stiff iron-on interfacing. Stick the embroidery on to thick, shiny card and cut into a star shape. Glue decorative braid around the edge of the fabric. Neaten the back with felt, adding a curtain ring hanger.

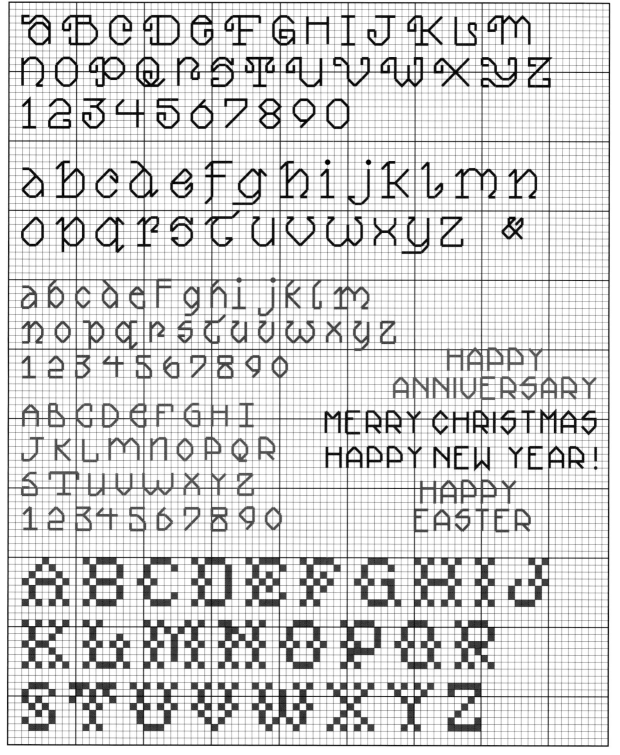

The alphabets and numbers charted here can be used to personalize the Calendar Teddies cards or to add names, greetings and messages to any of the designs in the book. Plan the letters or numbers on graph paper first to work out the space needed for the stitching. The spacing between letters is usually one or two squares. The colours for letters and numbers should match or tone with the design.

March and
April
DMC stranded cotton
Cross stitch (2 strands)

−	742
⅄	743
	744
■	816
T	869
	905
○	906
	907
	3829
•	blanc
	Kreinik
	028 citron

•	310
	312
×	334
╱	349
	351
	415
◄	602
←	603
>	605
╱	676
	677
	729

Backstitch (1 strand)
——— 310
——— 312
——— 905

French knots (2 strands)
● 310

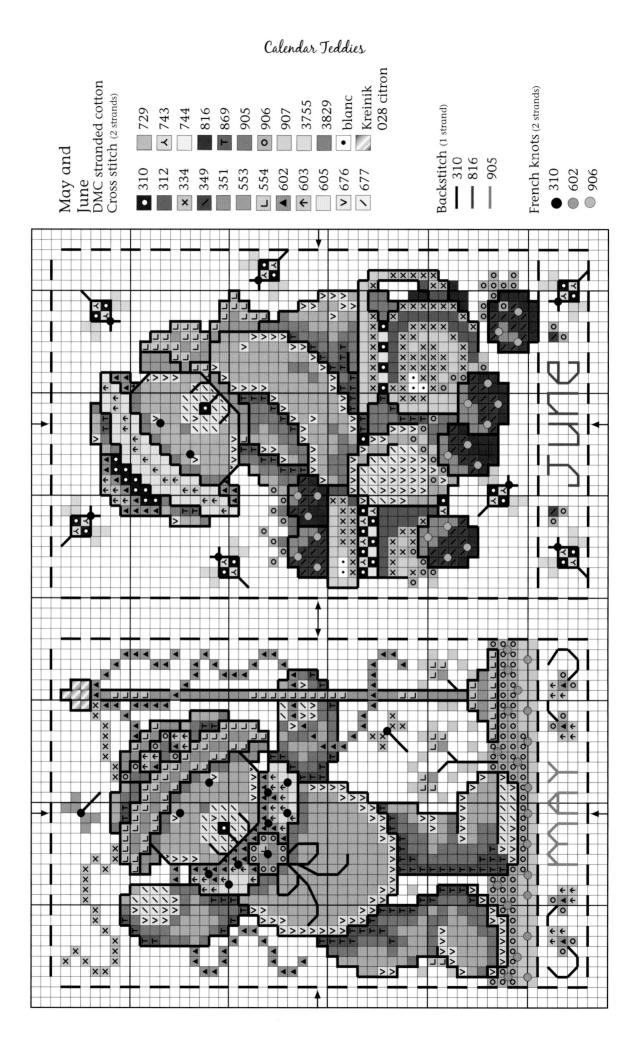

Calendar Teddies

May and June
DMC stranded cotton
Cross stitch (2 strands)

	729		729

Backstitch (1 strand)
— 310
— 816
— 905

French knots (2 strands)
● 310
● 602
● 906

JUNE

MAY

July and August

DMC stranded cotton
Cross stitch (2 strands)

310	●		— 742
312	■		⋏ 743
334	✕		744
349	╱		Ɪ 762
351			816
415			T 869
553			905
554	L		○ 906
602	◀		907
603	←		3755
605	⋁		3829
676	╱		• blanc
677			Kreinik
729			028 citron

Backstitch (1 strand)
———— 310
———— 816
———— 905
———— Kreinik 028

French knots (2 strands)
● 310
○ blanc

AUGUST

JULY

79

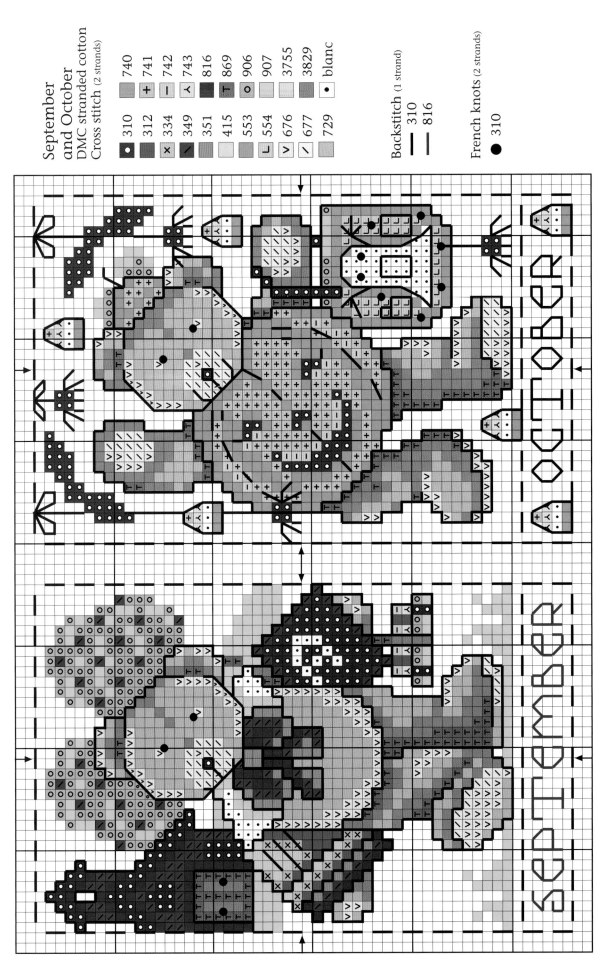

September and October
DMC stranded cotton
Cross stitch (2 strands)

	740
	741
	742
	743
	816
	869
	906
	907
	3755
	3829
	blanc

	310
	312
	334
	349
	351
	415
	553
	554
	676
	677
	729

Backstitch (1 strand)
— 310
— 816

French knots (2 strands)
● 310

OCTOBER

SEPTEMBER

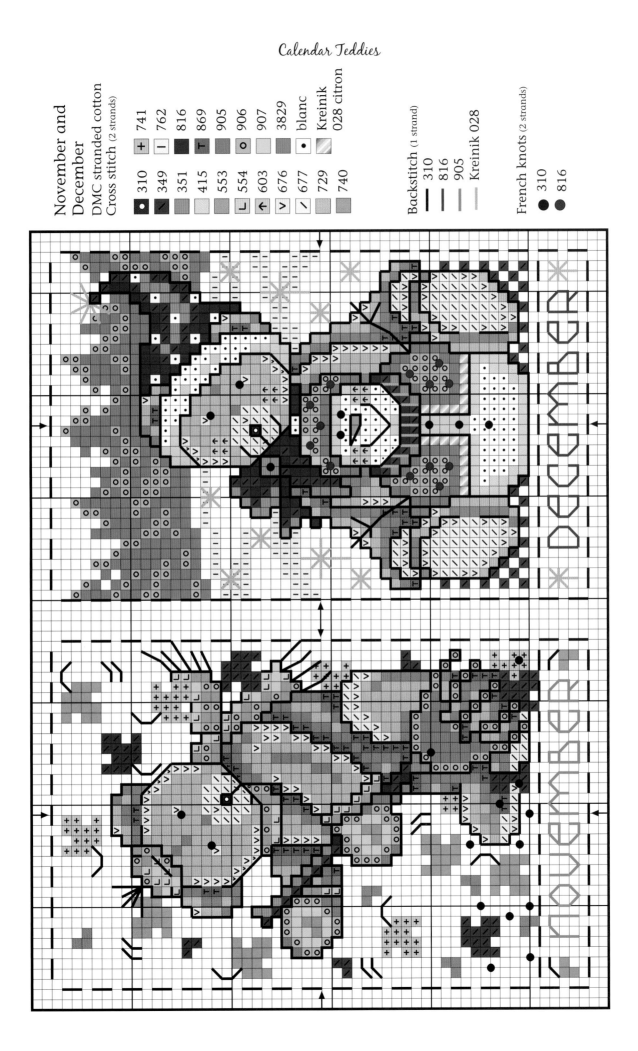

November and December

DMC stranded cotton
Cross stitch (2 strands)

+	741
I	762
	816
T	869
	905
o	906
	907
	3829
•	blanc
	Kreinik 028 citron

⊙	310
/	349
	351
	415
	553
L	554
←	603
V	676
⁄	677
	729
	740

Backstitch (1 strand)
— 310
— 816
— 905
— Kreinik 028

French knots (2 strands)
● 310
● 816

DECEMBER

NOVEMBER

Designed by Claire Crompton

Sweetheart Bears

Teddy bears have been the object of our affections for over

a century. Indeed, it is hard not to love them, with their soft fur,

the knowing twinkle in their eyes and their slight smile – and the fact that

they are always there for us.

The eight adorable little bears and their heartfelt messages in this chapter are

just perfect for sending love and affection at any time of year – you can use them

for birthday cards and gifts, for congratulations on anniversaries, at Christmas time,

Valentine's Day and a host of other occasions. The eight designs are all the same size

and so are interchangeable.

There are two cuddly cushions made from ultra-soft fleece which are sure to be

welcomed as gifts. Four of the designs have been made up as lovely greetings cards,

with various embellishments chosen to enhance the card mount and achieve a real

hand-crafted look. An attractive album to hold treasured memories can be tailored

to suit any wedding anniversary. And finally, for dark and chilly nights there is

a wonderfully cosy and easy to make hot-water bottle cover.

These dear little sweetheart bears adorning two bright cushions would make wonderful gifts – perfect to cuddle. There are lots of other ways you could use these versatile designs – see pages 90–91 for suggestions.

Sweetheart Cushions

The gorgeous little cushions shown on the previous page are made from soft fleece and are great for cuddling or are pretty enough just for display. See pages 90–91 for suggestions on using the designs in this chapter.

STITCH COUNT (each design)
59h x 56w
DESIGN SIZE
10.8 x 10.2cm (4¼ x 4in)
Finished pillow 25 x 25cm
(9¾ x 9¾in)
MATERIALS (for each cushion)
❀ White 14-count Aida
   20.3 x 20.3cm (8 x 8in)
❀ Tapestry needle size 24
❀ DMC stranded cotton (floss)
   as listed in the chart key
❀ Two 27 x 27cm (10½ x 10½in)
   pieces of fleece fabric
❀ 20 x 20cm (8 x 8in)
   lightweight iron-on
   interfacing
❀ Polyester stuffing

1 Prepare your fabric for work and mark the centre (see page 98). Follow the chart on page 92 and begin stitching from the centre of the chart and centre of the fabric, working over one Aida block.

2 Use two strands of stranded cotton (floss) for the cross stitches and then work the backstitches using the number of strands given in the chart key.

3 When all the stitching has been completed, fuse the iron-on interfacing to the wrong side of the patch according to the manufacturer's instructions. Trim the patch to 14cm (5½in) square, making sure the stitching is in the middle and there is the same amount of unworked Aida on all sides of the border. Turn under the raw edges 1cm (⅜in), tack (baste) down and press carefully.

4 Place the patch on to one of the fleece pieces, making sure it is centralized and straight. Sew the patch on to the fabric using two strands of stranded cotton to match your fleece and small running stitches (use the Aida blocks as a guide). Remove tacking (basting) thread.

5 Place the two pillow pieces right sides together and pin or tack (baste) together. Leaving one side open, stitch the pieces together using a 1cm (⅜in) seam. Trim the stitched corners diagonally to reduce bulk. Turn through to the right side and press the seams. Stuff the pillow, pushing the stuffing into the corners. To finish, turn under 1cm (⅜in) along the raw edges, pin the sides together and slipstitch the edge closed.

Anniversary Album

Celebrate a wedding anniversary with this photograph album to house all those wonderful memories. The number is easily changed using the chart provided. The design could be used for other gifts – see the suggestions on pages 90–91.

STITCH COUNT (each design)
59h x 56w
DESIGN SIZE
10.8 x 10.2cm (4¼ x 4in)
MATERIALS
❦ White 14-count Aida
20.3 x 20.3cm (8 x 8in)
❦ Tapestry needle size 24
❦ DMC stranded cotton (floss)
as listed in the chart key
❦ 14 x 14cm (5½ x 5½in)
square of red felt
❦ 20 x 20cm (8 x 8in)
lightweight iron-on
interfacing
❦ Photo album
❦ Double-sided adhesive tape

1 Prepare your fabric for work and mark the centre (see page 98). Follow the chart on page 93 and begin stitching from the centre of the chart and centre of the fabric, working over one Aida block.

2 Use two strands of stranded cotton (floss) for the cross stitches and then work the backstitches using the number of strands given in the chart key. Before stitching the central heart, use the numbers to chart an anniversary number. Place it on the two blue lines in the heart and cross stitch the number using two strands of 451. Complete the heart and backstitch the numbers.

3 When all the stitching has been completed, fuse the iron-on interfacing to the wrong side of the patch according to the manufacturer's instructions. Trim the patch to 14cm (5½in) square, making sure the stitching is in the middle and there is the same amount of unworked Aida on all sides of the border. Turn under the raw edges 1cm (⅜in), tack (baste) down and press carefully.

4 Place the patch on to the square of felt, making sure it is centralised and straight. Sew the patch on to the felt using two strands of 319 stranded cotton (floss) and small running stitches (use the Aida blocks as a guide). Remove tacking (basting) thread.

5 To finish, stick double-sided tape on the back of the felt, around the edges and across the middle. Peel off the backing tape and stick the patch on to the front of the album, making sure it is in the middle and straight.

Sweetheart Bear Cards

These four delightful cards are a wonderful way to send your love and affection to your family and friends. Simple but stylish embellishments add a professional look. There are many other ways you could use the designs – see pages 90–91 for ideas.

STITCH COUNT (each design)
59h x 56w
DESIGN SIZE
10.8 x 10.2cm (4¼ x 4in)
MATERIALS (for each card)
❀ White 14-count Aida
   20.3 x 20.3cm (8 x 8in)
❀ Tapestry needle size 24
❀ DMC stranded cotton (floss)
   as listed in the chart key
❀ Double-fold card with
   12.5cm (5in) aperture
❀ Double-sided adhesive tape
❀ Card embellishments
   (see Suppliers)

1 Prepare your fabric for work and mark the centre (see page 98). Follow the charts on pages 94 and 95 and begin stitching from the centre of the chart and fabric. Work over one Aida block.

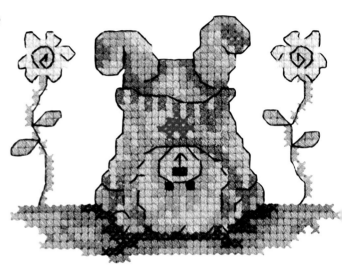

2 Use two strands of stranded cotton (floss) for the cross stitches and then work the backstitches using the number of strands given in the chart key.

3 Mount your work into the card following the instructions on page 101. Decorate the card mount with embellishments of your choice. Stickers and rub-ons have been used, plus some three-dimensional toppers. Your local craft store should have plenty to choose from (see also Suppliers on page 104).

The winter of 1906 was a bitterly cold one and in response, the well-known toy-making company Steiff produced a teddy hot-water bottle. Surviving examples are very rare as only 90 were made.

Fuzzy Feelings Hot-Water Bottle

Here's another snugly project to keep you warm and toasty on cold evenings. The hot-water bottle cover is simple to make and will be really useful to display many of the cross stitch designs from this book. Take care with hot-water bottles if being used for a child.

STITCH COUNT
59h x 56w
DESIGN SIZE
10.8 x 10.2cm (4¼ x 4in)

MATERIALS
✿ White 14-count Aida
 20.3 x 20.3cm (8 x 8in)

✿ Tapestry needle size 24

✿ DMC stranded cotton (floss)
 as listed in the chart key

✿ Light mauve fleece
 46 x 46cm (18 x 18in)

✿ Lightweight iron-on
 interfacing 20 x 20cm
 (8 x 8in)

✿ Velcro 1.3cm (½in)

✿ Child's or mini hot-water
 bottle 23cm (9in) high
 x 14.5cm (5¾in) wide

✿ Sheet of tracing paper

✿ Pins

✿ Matching sewing thread

1 Prepare your fabric for work and mark the centre (see page 98). Follow the chart on page 93 and begin stitching from the centre of the chart and centre of the fabric, working over one Aida block. Use two strands of stranded cotton (floss) for the cross stitches and then work the backstitches using the number of strands given in the chart key.

2 When all the stitching has been completed, fuse the iron-on interfacing to the wrong side of the patch (see page 101). Trim the patch to 14cm (5½in) square, making sure the stitching is central with the same amount of unworked Aida on all sides of the border. Turn under raw edges 1cm (⅜in), tack (baste) down and press carefully.

3 Begin the cover as follows. Place the tracing paper over each template on page 96 and 97, draw around and cut out the pattern pieces. Pin these on to the fleece fabric and cut out a front, upper and lower back. Place the embroidered patch on to the front of the cover, centralizing it on the widest part and straight. Sew the patch in place using two strands of 3041 stranded cotton (floss) and small running stitches (use the Aida blocks as a guide). Remove tacking (basting) thread.

4 Make up the cover by first turning under 2cm (¾in) of the raw edges along the top edge of the lower back and along the bottom edge of the upper back. Tack down and press. Stitch along each edge through both thicknesses 1cm (⅜in) away from the fold. Remove tacking (basting) thread. Place the front flat with right side uppermost, place the lower back on to the front with right sides together, matching the edges. Place the upper back on top, matching the edges. Upper and lower backs will overlap. Tack in position. Using matching sewing thread, stitch around the edge of the cover using a 1cm (⅜in) seam allowance. Remove tacking. Turn the cover through to the right side, pushing out the corners and curves, and press seams carefully. Sew the Velcro into the centre of the overlap and insert the hot-water bottle.

Bearing Gifts...

Go wild with a whole range of ideas for using the darling bears from this chapter. Create patches to adorn clothes and household items, mix the designs up with patchwork or just stitch them for greetings cards. Alphabets charted on page 75 could be used to personalize the designs.

For a very special anniversary why not find a special frame and stitch these two loving bears? A stained-glass frame in delicate colours would look wonderful or try an embossed silver or gold frame for a 25th or 50th wedding anniversary.

You can create a bookmark gift for a dear friend in no time by stitching just a teddy with a few hearts on a strip of Aida band. Hem the top straight and the bottom into a point. A little silver bell makes a nice finishing touch.

Be adventurous with your cross stitch and use several of the sweetheart teddies to create a gorgeous patchwork bag. Choose some pretty, chintzy fabrics and sew nine squares together as shown here. Make up into a simple bag with ribbon tape or webbing for handles and add some matching embellishments.

Make a fun
wall hanging for a child's
room. Stitch one of the teddy
designs, perhaps on an unusual
shade and fuse it to some pretty
print fabric. Cut some stiff card and fix
the stitching around the card with glue
or double-sided tape. Frame the design
with an edging of ribbon or braid and
stitch on some bright jingle bells
along the lower edge. Make a
hanger from satin ribbon
tied in a big bow.

The cosy
cushions shown on page
83 can be made in different
shapes – try circles, stars or the
heart shape shown here. Make the
cushion from soft fleece or woolly
fabric for maximum snuggliness
and sew the patch in place with
an edging of braid or even
bright beads.

The bear
designs in this chapter
are so cute you are sure to
want to use them on all sorts of
containers, boxes and bags. There
are many ready-made cosmetic
and toiletries bags available from
high-street stores, which can be
embellished with a teddy patch.
Add a matching tassel
to the zip pull for an
extra flourish.

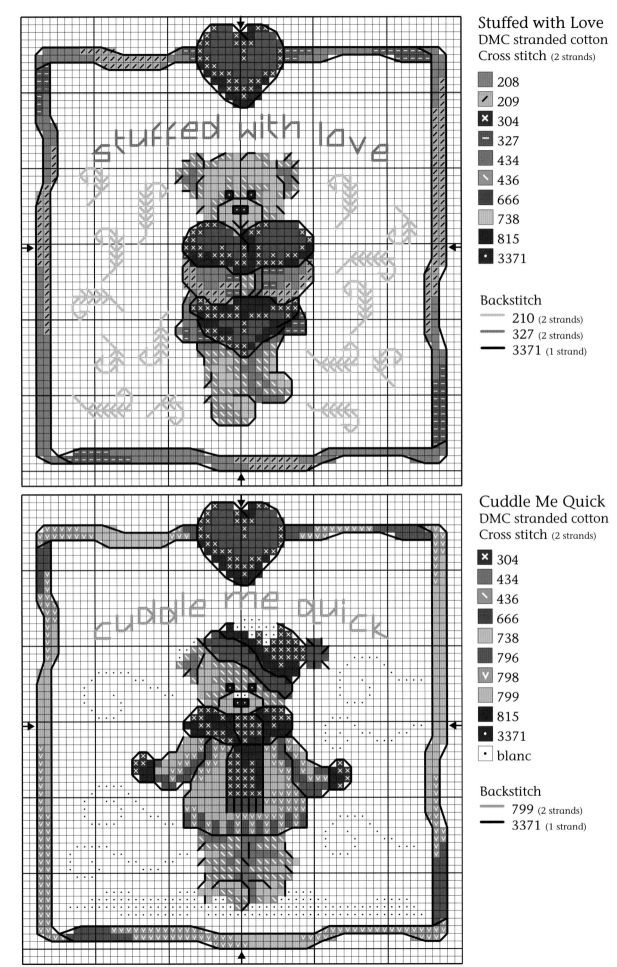

Stuffed with Love
DMC stranded cotton
Cross stitch (2 strands)

- 208
- / 209
- × 304
- – 327
- 434
- \ 436
- 666
- 738
- 815
- · 3371

Backstitch

- 210 (2 strands)
- 327 (2 strands)
- 3371 (1 strand)

Cuddle Me Quick
DMC stranded cotton
Cross stitch (2 strands)

- × 304
- 434
- \ 436
- 666
- 738
- 796
- V 798
- 799
- 815
- · 3371
- · blanc

Backstitch

- 799 (2 strands)
- 3371 (1 strand)

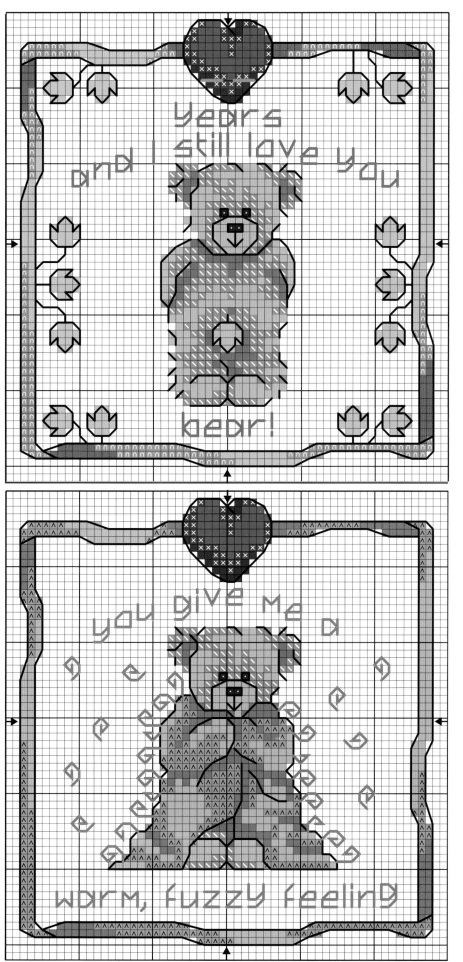

I Still Love You Bear
DMC stranded cotton
Cross stitch (2 strands)

✖	304	╲	436
	319		666
∩	320		738
	368		815
	415	•	3371
	434		

Backstitch
— 319 (2 strands)
— 3371 (1 strand)

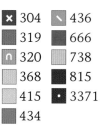

Change the numbers in the
central heart to your choice.
Position on the blue lines

You Give Me a
Warm Fuzzy Feeling
DMC stranded cotton
Cross stitch (2 strands)

✖	304
	434
╲	436
	666
	738
	815
	3041
∧	3042
•	3371
	3743

Backstitch
— 3041 (2 strands)
— 3371 (1 strand)

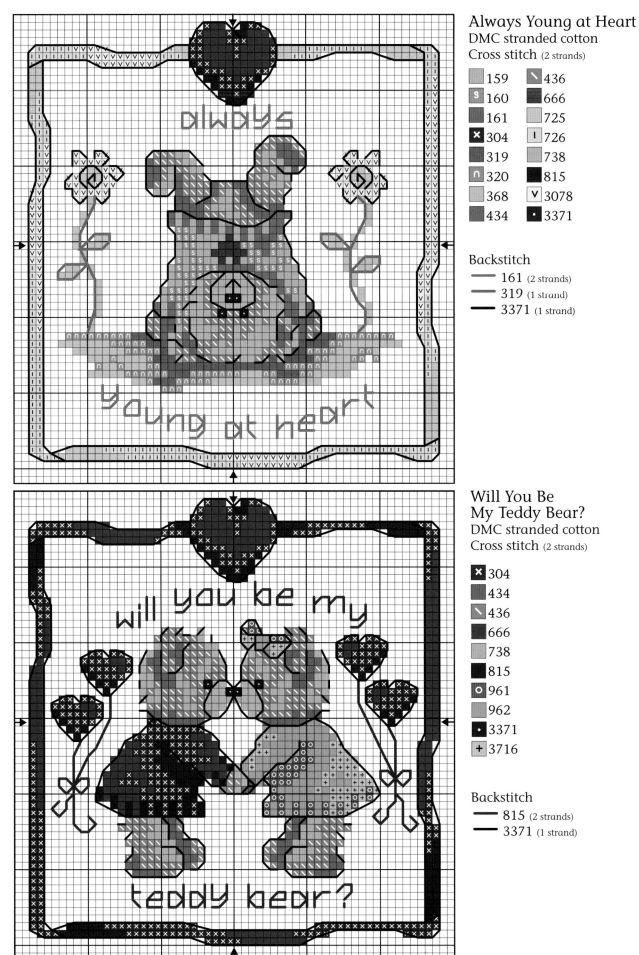

Always Young at Heart
DMC stranded cotton
Cross stitch (2 strands)

▨	159	◣	436
s	160		666
	161		725
✖	304	I	726
	319		738
∩	320		815
	368	V	3078
	434	•	3371

Backstitch

— 161 (2 strands)
— 319 (1 strand)
— 3371 (1 strand)

Will You Be My Teddy Bear?
DMC stranded cotton
Cross stitch (2 strands)

✖	304
	434
◣	436
	666
	738
	815
⊙	961
	962
•	3371
+	3716

Backstitch

— 815 (2 strands)
— 3371 (1 strand)

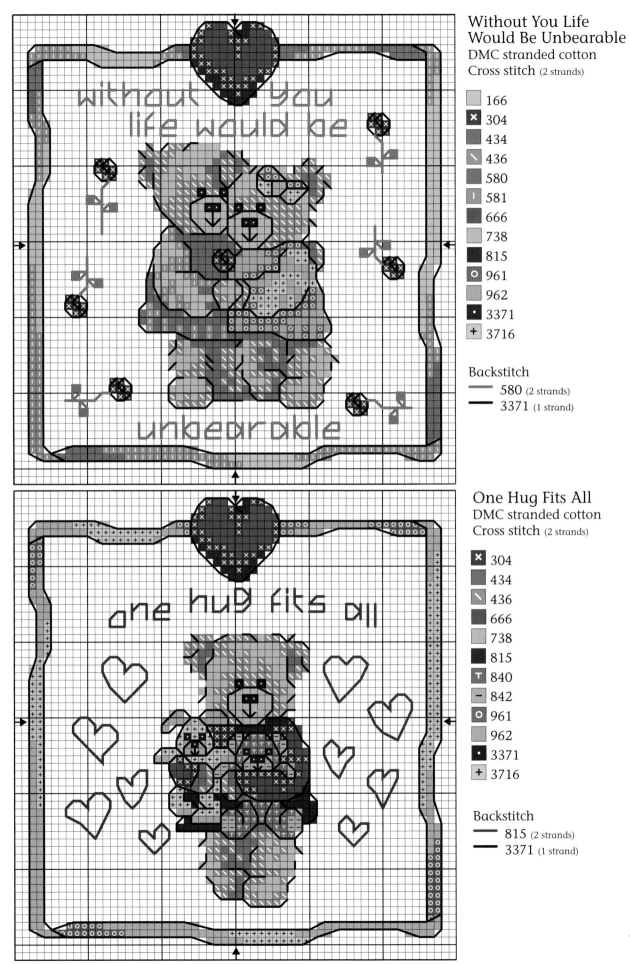

Without You Life Would Be Unbearable

DMC stranded cotton
Cross stitch (2 strands)

	166
✗	304
	434
＼	436
	580
｜	581
	666
	738
	815
⊙	961
	962
•	3371
＋	3716

Backstitch

— 580 (2 strands)
— 3371 (1 strand)

One Hug Fits All

DMC stranded cotton
Cross stitch (2 strands)

✗	304
	434
＼	436
	666
	738
	815
T	840
−	842
⊙	961
	962
•	3371
＋	3716

Backstitch

— 815 (2 strands)
— 3371 (1 strand)

Hot-Water Bottle Cover Templates
(actual size)

Front

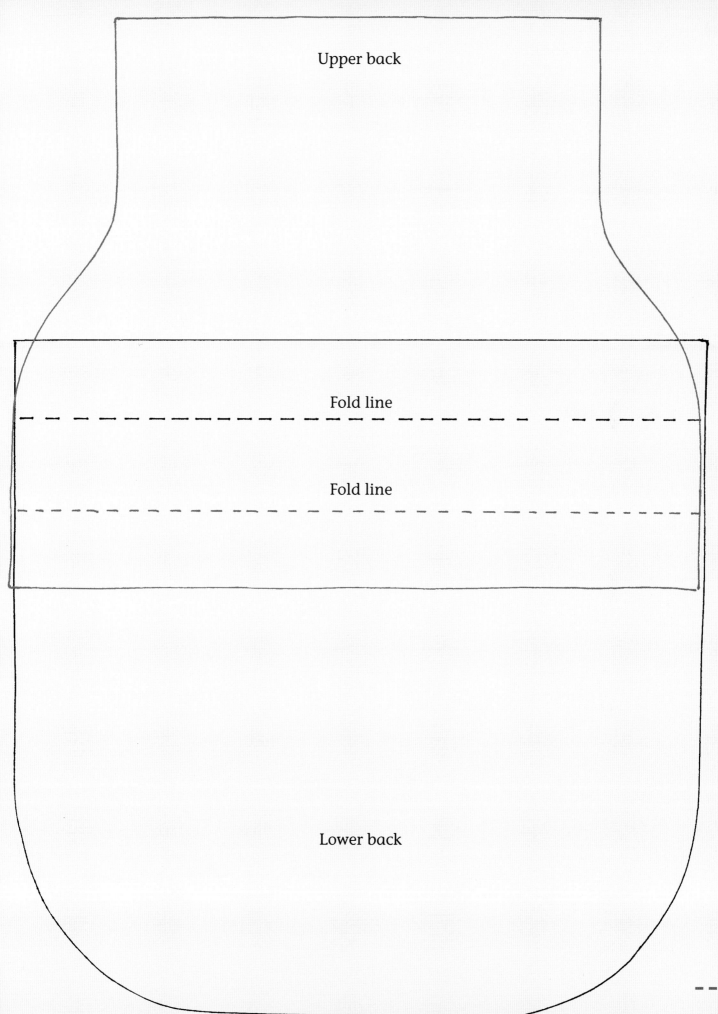

Upper back

Fold line

Fold line

Lower back

Materials, Techniques & Stitches

This section is useful to beginners as it describes the materials and equipment required and the basic techniques and stitches needed to work the projects. Framing pictures and mounting work in cards is described on page 101. Refer to Suppliers for useful addresses.

Materials

Fabrics

The designs in this book have been worked over one block of 14-count Aida. You could also work the designs on 28-count evenweave, working over two fabric threads. If you change the gauge (count) of the material, that is the number of holes per inch, then the size of the finished work will alter accordingly – see Calculating Stitch Count and Design Size.

Threads

The projects have been stitched with DMC stranded embroidery cotton (floss) but you could match the colours to other thread ranges – ask at your local needlework store. The six-stranded skeins can easily be split into separate threads. The project instructions and chart keys tell you how many strands to use. Some designs also use metallic threads.

Needles

Tapestry needles are available in different sizes and are used for cross stitch as they have a rounded point and do not snag fabric.

Scissors

You will need two pairs of scissors: a pair of dressmaking shears for cutting fabrics and a small pair of sharp-pointed embroidery scissors for cutting and trimming threads.

Frames

It is a matter of personal preference as to whether you use an embroidery frame or hoop to keep your fabric taut while stitching. Generally speaking, working with a frame helps to keep the tension even and prevent distortion, while working without a frame is faster and less cumbersome. There are various types on the market – look in your local needlework store.

Techniques

Preparing the Fabric

Spending a little time preparing your embroidery fabric before stitching will save time and trouble in the long run.

❀ Before starting work, check the design size given with each project and make sure that this is the size you require for your finished embroidery. Your fabric must be larger than the finished design size to allow for making up, so allow 13cm (5in) to both dimensions when stitching a picture and 7.5cm (3in) for smaller projects.

❀ Before beginning to stitch, neaten the fabric edges either by hemming or zigzagging to prevent fraying as you work.

❀ Find the centre of the fabric. This is important regardless of which direction you work from, in order to stitch the design centrally on the fabric. To find the centre, fold the fabric in half horizontally and then vertically, then tack (baste) along the folds (or use tailor's chalk). The centre point is where the two lines meet. This point on the fabric should correspond to the centre point on the chart. Remove these lines on completion of the work.

Calculating Stitch Count and Design Size

Each project gives the stitch count and finished design size but if you want to work the design on a different count fabric you will need to re-calculate the finished size. Being able to work out the eventual size of a design means that you can decide how much fabric you need for a particular project or whether a design will fit a specific picture frame or card aperture.

Stitch count To work out the stitch count, first count how many stitches there are along the height of a design and then along the width (don't forget to count any backstitches or French knots too on the outer edge of a design). Fig 1 shows a design that is 55 stitches high and 35 stitches wide.

Finished design size To work out the finished design size, divide each of the stitch count numbers by the fabric count of the embroidery fabric you want to use. For example, the charted design shown is 55 stitches high x 35 stitches wide and was worked on 14-count Aida. So, 55 ÷ 14 = 3.9

inches (round this up to 4 inches), and 35 ÷ 14 = 2½ inches. So the finished stitched design will be 4 x 2½in (10.2 x 6.3cm). The same design worked on 18-count Aida would have a smaller finished size of 3in x 2in (7.6 x 5cm), because 18-count fabric is finer.

When calculating design sizes for evenweave fabrics, divide the fabric count by 2 before you start, because evenweave is worked over two threads not one block as with Aida.

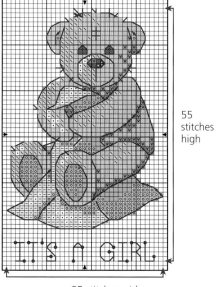

55 stitches high

35 stitches wide

Fig 1 Working out the stitch count of a cross stitch design or motif

Using Charts and Keys

The charts in this book are easy to work from. Each square on the chart represents one stitch. Each coloured square, or coloured square with a symbol, represents a thread colour, with the code number given in the chart key. A few of the designs use fractional stitches (three-quarter cross stitches) to give more definition to the design. Solid coloured lines show where backstitches or long stitches are to be worked. French knots are shown by coloured circles.

Each complete chart has arrows at the sides to show the centre point, which you could mark with a pen. Where a chart has been split over several pages, the key is repeated. For your own use, you could colour photocopy and enlarge charts.

Starting and Finishing

It is always a good idea to start and finish work correctly, to create the neatest effect and avoid ugly bumps and threads trailing across the back of work. To finish off thread, pass the needle through several nearby stitches on the wrong side of the work, then cut the thread off, close to the fabric.

Knotless Loop Start

You can start this way if you are intending to stitch with an even number of strands, i.e. 2, 4, or 6. Cut the stranded cotton roughly twice the length you would normally need and separate one strand. Double this strand and thread your needle with the two ends. Pierce your fabric from the wrong side where you intend to place your first stitch, leaving the looped end at the back of the work. Return the needle to the wrong side after forming a half cross stitch and pass it through the waiting loop. You can now begin to stitch.

Away Waste Knot Start

Start this way if working with an odd number of strands or when using variegated threads. Thread your needle and make a knot at the end. Take the needle and thread through from the front of the fabric to the back and come up again about 2.5cm (1in) away from the knot. Now either start cross stitching and work towards the knot, cutting it off when the threads are anchored, or thread the end into your needle and finish off under some completed stitches.

Washing and Pressing

If you need to wash your finished embroidery, first make sure the stranded cottons are colourfast by washing them in tepid water and mild soap. Rinse well and lay out flat to dry completely before beginning to stitch with them. Wash completed embroideries in the same way and avoid wringing wet stitching. Iron on a medium setting, covering the ironing board with a thick layer of towelling. Place the stitching right side down into the towelling and press gently.

Stitches

Backstitch

Backstitches are used to give definition to parts of a design and to outline areas. Many of the charts use different coloured backstitches. Some designs use a 'sketchy' backstitch style, where the backstitch doesn't always outline the cross stitches exactly.

To work backstitch follow the diagram below, bringing the needle up at 1 and down at 2. Then bring the needle up again at 3, and so on.

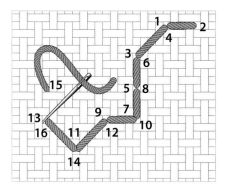

Fig 2 Working backstitch

Cross Stitch

A cross stitch can be worked singly over one block of Aida (Fig 3a) or over two threads of linen or evenweave fabric (Fig 3b).

To make a cross stitch over one block of Aida, bring the needle up through the fabric at the bottom left side of the stitch (number 1 on Fig 3a) and cross diagonally to the top right corner (2). Push the needle through the hole and bring up through the bottom right corner (3), crossing the fabric diagonally to the top left corner to finish the stitch (4). To work the next stitch, come up through the bottom right corner of the first stitch and repeat the sequence.

You can also work cross stitch in two journeys by working a number of half cross stitches in a line and completing the stitches on the return journey. For neat work, always finish the cross stitch with the top stitches lying in the same diagonal direction.

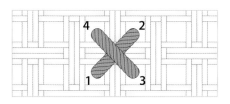

Fig 3a Working a single cross stitch on Aida fabric

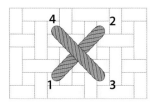

Fig 3b Working a single cross stitch on linen or evenweave fabric

French Knot

French knots have been used as highlights and details in some of the designs, in various colours. To work, follow Fig 4, bringing the needle and thread up through the fabric at the exact place where the knot is to be positioned. Wrap the thread once or twice around the needle (according to the project instructions), holding the thread firmly close to the needle, then twist the needle back through the fabric as close as possible to where it first emerged. Holding the knot down carefully, pull the thread through to the back leaving the knot on the surface, securing it with one small stitch on the back.

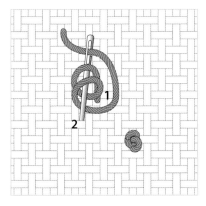

Fig 4 Working a French knot

Three-quarter Cross Stitch

Three-quarter cross stitches give more detail and the illusion of curves to a design. They are shown by a triangle within a square on the charts. Working three-quarter cross stitches is easier on evenweave fabric than Aida (see Fig 5). To work on Aida, make a half cross stitch from corner to corner and then work a quarter stitch from the other corner into the centre of the Aida square, piercing the fabric.

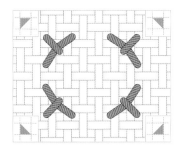

Fig 5 Working three-quarter cross stitch

Tips for Perfect Stitching

Counted cross stitch is one of the easiest forms of counted embroidery. Following these useful pointers will help you to produce neat work.

✿ Before starting, check the design size given with each project and make sure that this is the size you require for your finished embroidery. The fabric you are stitching on should be at least 5cm (2in) larger all round than the finished size of the stitching, to allow for making up.

✿ Organize your threads before you start a project as this will help to avoid confusion later. Put the threads required for a particular project on an organizer (available from craft shops) and always include the manufacturer's name and the shade number. You can make your own thread organizer by punching holes along one side of a piece of thick card.

✿ When you have cut the length of stranded cotton (floss) you need, usually about 46cm (18in), separate out all the strands before taking the number you need, realigning them and threading your needle.

✿ If using a hoop, avoid placing it over worked stitches and remove it from the fabric at the end of a stitching session.

✿ For neat cross stitching, work the top stitches so they all face in the same direction.

✿ If your thread begins to twist, turn the work upside down and let the needle spin for a few moments.

✿ If adding a backstitch outline, add it after the cross stitch has been completed to prevent the solid line of the backstitch being broken.

Making Up

Making up the projects is described in the relevant chapters but some general techniques are described here.

Using Iron-on Interfacing

Iron-on interfacing can be used to stiffen and stabilize your cross stitch embroidery and allow the edges to be cut without fraying. Adhesive webbing is available as single-sided and double-sided, i.e., with glue on one side or both, allowing you to fuse the embroidery to another fabric. This means that cross stitch designs can be used to decorate all sorts of ready-made items.

Cut the interfacing or adhesive webbing roughly to the size of the embroidery fabric and fuse it to the back of the embroidery with a medium iron, placing the embroidery face down into some thick towels. Once fused, trim to size.

Using Ready-Made Items

Many of the projects in the book can be displayed in ready-made items such as coasters, pen pots and trinket pots. There are various manufacturers supplying such items (see Suppliers). Smaller pieces of embroidery can be backed with an iron-on interfacing to firm up the fabric and prevent wrinkling. The embroidery is then trimmed to the correct size and mounted in the item following the manufacturer's instructions.

Mounting and Framing

It really is best to take large samplers and pictures to a professional framer, where you can choose from a wide variety of mounts and frames that will best enhance your work. The framer will be able to stretch the fabric correctly and cut mounts accurately.

If you intend to mount the work yourself, use acid-free mounting board in a colour that will not show through the embroidery.

1 Cut a piece of mount board to fit the frame aperture (draw around the frame's backing board). Using double-sided tape, stick a piece of wadding (batting) to the mount board and trim the wadding to the same size using a sharp craft knife.

2 Lay the embroidery right side up on to the wadding, making sure the design is central and straight, matching a fabric thread along the edges. Push pins through at the four corners and along the edges to mark the position. Trim the fabric to leave 5cm (2in) all around.

3 Turn the embroidery and mount board over together. Stick double-sided tape around the edges of the board to a depth of 5cm (2in) and peel off the backing. Fold the excess fabric back, pressing down firmly to stick the fabric to the board, adding more tape to neaten the corners. Remove the pins and reassemble the frame with the embroidery in it. It is not necessary to use the glass; this often flattens the stitches when they are pushed against it.

Mounting Work into Cards

Many of the designs can be made up into cards and there are many styles of card mounts available today. Some are simple single-fold cards, while others are pre-folded with three sections, the middle one having a window or aperture for your embroidery.

Mounting Work on a Single-Fold Card

1 Back the embroidery with iron-on interfacing to stabilize the edges and then trim the embroidery to the size required. If you want a fringe around the stitching, cut the interfacing slightly smaller, leaving two or three extra rows all round.

2 Attach the embroidery to the front of your card using double-sided adhesive tape. For a fringe, pull away the outer fabric threads to form the fringe and fix in place on the card with double-sided tape. If not fringed, the edge of the fabric could be decorated with braid or ribbon.

Mounting Work in a Double-Fold Card

1 To mount embroidery in a ready-made, double-fold card, position the embroidery in the window space – the fabric should be at least 2.5cm (1in) larger than the aperture all round, so trim it if necessary.

2 On the inside of the card, place strips of double-sided adhesive tape around the aperture, peel off the backing and secure the embroidery.

3 Fold over the third of the card to cover. This can be secured with double-sided tape for a neater finish. Embellish the card mount as desired.

The Designers

Sue Cook

Sue has been a freelance designer since 1992 and in that time she has worked for all the major UK stitching magazines and created hundreds of memorable designs. Sue has authored five books for David & Charles including *Crafting Cross Stitch Cards*. She lives in Newport, South Wales, with her husband Ade.

Claire Crompton

Claire studied knitwear design at college before joining the design team at DMC, and finally going freelance. Claire's work has appeared in several magazines, including *Cross Stitch Magic*. Her designs also feature in six David & Charles books: *Cross Stitch Greetings Cards*, *Cross Stitch Alphabets*, *Cross Stitch Angels*, *Cross Stitch Fairies*, *Magical Cross Stitch* and *Quick to Stitch Cross Stitch Cards*, and in her solo books *Cross Stitch Card Collection*, *Picture Your Pet in Cross Stitch* and *Christmas Cross Stitch*, also published by David & Charles. Claire lives in Gunnislake, Cornwall.

Joan Elliott

Joan has been creating needlework designs for over 30 years, enchanting stitching enthusiasts the world over with her unique humour and charm. Design Works Crafts Inc in the United States (see Suppliers) produce kits of many of her designs and she remains their leading artist. Her debut book for David & Charles, *A Cross Stitcher's Oriental Odyssey*, was followed by *Cross Stitch Teddies*, *Cross Stitch Sentiments & Sayings*, *Joan Elliott's Native American Cross Stitch*, *Cross Stitch Wit & Wisdom* and *Cross Stitch a Woman's World*. Joan divides her time between Brooklyn, New York and Vermont.

Michaela Learner

Michaela is an experienced needlewoman, having had a passion for all aspects of decorative needlecraft as far back as she will admit to remembering. She has contributed designs to books and magazines and has recently had her first book of cross stitch designs published. Michaela lives and works from her home in Cardiff, Wales, UK.

Joanne Sanderson

Joanne has been designing cross stitch projects for many years and contributes to many popular needlecraft magazines. She also produces designs for DMC kits and publications. Her designs appeared in *Magical Cross Stitch* and *Cross Stitch Cuties* for David & Charles. She has also authored a papercraft title for David & Charles, *3D Rubber Stamping*. Joanne lives in South Yorkshire with her daughter.

Lesley Teare

Lesley trained as a textile designer, with a degree in printed and woven textiles. For some years she has been one of DMC's leading designers and her designs have also featured in many of the cross stitch magazines. Lesley has contributed to five books for David & Charles – *Cross Stitch Greetings Cards, Cross Stitch Alphabets, Cross Stitch Angels, Cross Stitch Fairies* and *Magical Cross Stitch*. She has also authored four solo books – *101 Weekend Cross Stitch Gifts, Travel the World in Cross Stitch, Oriental Cross Stitch* and *Fantasy Cross Stitch*. Lesley lives in Hitcham, Suffolk.

Suppliers

UK

CardArt Ltd
Kensington Industrial Park,
Southport PR9 0NY
www.cardart.co.uk
For card labels with gold writing on cream in Sweetheart Bears chapter

Coats Crafts UK
PO Box 22, Lingfield House, McMullen
Road, Darlington, Co. Durham DL1 1YQ
Tel: 01325 394237 (consumer helpline)
www.coatscrafts.co.uk
For Anchor stranded cotton (floss) and other embroidery supplies

Creative Crafts & Needlework
18 High Street, Totnes, Devon TQ9 5RY
Tel: 01803 866002
www.creative-crafts-needlework.co.uk
For a general needlework, craft and patchwork supplies, including DMC and Anchor threads

Craft Creations Ltd
Ingersoll House, Delamare Road,
Cheshunt, Hertfordshire, EN8 9HD
Tel: 01992 781900
Email: enquiries@craftcreations.com
www.craftcreations.com
For card mounts and card-making accessories. The Woodland Greetings cards used cream double-fold cards with a circular aperture (code AP03U)

Crafty Bitz
22 Seymour Gardens, Ilford, Essex IG1 3LN
www.craftybitz.co.uk
For the valentine hearts in the Sweetheart Bears chapter (Ref VS004 3D) and the To You paper label (Ref DS126)

DMC Creative World Ltd
1st Floor Compass Building, Feldspar
Close, Enderby, Leicestershire LE19 4SD
Tel: 0116 275 4000
Fax: 0116 275 4020
www.dmccreative.co.uk
For embroidery fabrics, stranded cotton, metallic threads and items with cross stitch inserts, such as bibs

Framecraft Miniatures Ltd
Unit 3, Isis House, Lindon Road,
Brownhills, West Midlands WS8 7BW
Tel/fax (UK): 01543 360842
Tel (international): 44 1543 453154
Email: sales@framecraft.com
www.framecraft.com
For coasters, pen pots, trinket bowls and other items with cross stitch inserts

Heritage Stitchcraft
Redbrook Lane, Brereton, Rugeley,
Staffordshire WS15 1QU
Tel: 01889 575256
Email: enquiries@heritagestitchcraft.com
www.heritagestitchcraft.com
For Zweigart fabrics and other embroidery supplies

Impressive Crafts Ltd
Unit 1 James Watt Close, Gapton Hall Ind
Est, Great Yarmouth, Norfolk NR31 0NX
Tel: 01493 441166
www.impressivecrafts.com
Email: sales@impresscards.co.uk
For card blanks and craft supplies

Madeira Threads (UK) Ltd
PO Box 6, Thirsk, North Yorkshire YO7 3YX
Tel: 01845 524880
Email: info@madeira.co.uk
www.madeira.co.uk
For Madeira stranded cottons and other embroidery supplies. For a thread conversion chart ring 01765 640003

Papermania
Design Objectives Ltd, Wimborne,
Dorset BH21 6SU
www.papermania.co.uk
For clear stickers of Happy Birthday, numbers and presents in Sweetheart Bears chapter (Ref PMA 654 party selection)

USA

Joann Stores, Inc
5555 Darrow Road, Hudson Ohio
Tel: 1 888 739 4120
Email: guest service@jo-annstores.com
www.joann.com
For general needlework supplies (mail order and shops across the US)

Kreinik Manufacturing Company, Inc
3106 Timanus Lane, Suite 101, Baltimore,
MD 21244
Tel: 1800 537 2166
Email: kreinik@kreinik.com
www.kreinik.com
For a wide range of metallic threads and blending filaments

MCG Textiles
13845 Magnolia Avenue, Chino,
CA 91710
Tel: 909 591 6351
www.mcgtextiles.com
For cross stitch fabrics and pre-finished items

M & J Buttons
1000 Sixth Avenue, New York, NY 10018
Tel: 212 391 6200
www.mjtrim.com
For beads, buttons, ribbons and trimmings

Mill Hill, a division of Wichelt Imports Inc
N162 Hwy 35, Stoddard WI 54658
Tel: 608 788 4600
Email: millhill@millhill.com
www.millhill.com
For Mill Hill beads and a US source for Framecraft products

Acknowledgments

The publishers would like to thank the following designers for their contributions: Sue Cook, Claire Crompton, Joan Elliott, Michaela Learner, Joanne Sanderson and Lesley Teare. Thanks also go to Lin Clements for managing the project, editing the title and preparing the charts and ideas artworks.

Sue Cook would like to thank Cheryl Brown for including her designs and having them stitched by Michaela. Claire Crompton would like to thank Cara Ackerman at DMC for supplying the threads and fabric. Joan Elliott would like to offer heartfelt thanks to her wonderful model stitchers, Bev Ritter and Judi Trochimiak, who somehow always manage to meet her deadlines, to DMC Creative World for providing her with their beautiful colours and warmest thanks to Lin Clements for her expert editing on the entire book. Michaela Learner thanks DMC Creative World for threads and fabric and Coats Crafts UK for their Ophir gold thread. Joanne Sanderson would like to thank Cara Ackerman at DMC Creative World for supplying the materials for her projects. Lesley Teare would like to thank her stitcher Tina Godwin and Heritage Stitchcraft for the lovely Zweigart fabrics.

Index

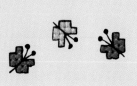